INDO-CHINA

om Penh
Saigon

BALI and ANGKOR
A map for the
readers guidance
Scale: 200 miles to 1 inch.

CHINA SEA

BORNEO

CRATAVIA
Buitenzorg
JAVA
Samarang
Jokarta
TAKARTA
TABAIA
Singaraja
BALI I.

Bali and Angkor

Books by
GEOFFREY GORER

The Revolutionary Ideas of the Marquis de Sade
Africa Dances

The Towers of the Bayon

Bali and Angkor

A 1930s pleasure trip
looking at Life and Death

Geoffrey Gorer

SINGAPORE OXFORD NEW YORK
OXFORD UNIVERSITY PRESS
1986

Oxford University Press

Oxford   New York   Toronto
Petaling Jaya   Singapore   Hong Kong   Tokyo
Delhi   Bombay   Calcutta   Madras   Karachi
Nairobi   Dar es Salaam   Cape Town
Melbourne   Auckland

and associates in
Beirut   Berlin   Ibadan   Nicosia

OXFORD is a trademark of Oxford University Press

© Leslie G. T. Mitchell 1936

Originally published by Michael Joseph Ltd. 1936
First issued as an Oxford University Press paperback 1986

ISBN 0 19 582692 2

Printed in Malaysia by Peter Chong Printers Sdn. Bhd.
Published by Oxford University Pte. Ltd.,
Unit 221, Ubi Avenue 4, Singapore 1440

FOR
MY MOTHER
WITH LOVE

CONTENTS

LIST OF ILLUSTRATIONS

*All photos save those marked by an asterisk were
taken by the Author.*

FOREWORD

In the first months of 1935 I was taken for a three months' pleasure trip to Sumatra, Java, Bali, and Indo-China, with short stops in the Malay States and Siam. I travelled in considerable luxury; there were everywhere excellent hotels and (save in Indo-China) very good cars and roads. Except for the fact that we travelled rather slowly, our journey differed little from that of other tourists; I saw little that other tourists couldn't see. Such a method of travelling has obvious disadvantages; although I learned enough Malay to get along with—it is the easiest language in the world—my intercourse with the natives of the different places I went to was slight and intermittent. I naturally talked as much as I could with the chauffeurs and servants I had anything to do with, for they were the most interesting people in the neighbourhood; and whenever I had the opportunity I used to talk to strangers in the streets or the country; but after these encounters I always went back to the hotel or the car. Now one of the chief disadvantages of living in hotels and cars is that everything seen through their windows is likely to be couleur de rose; Europeans or Americans enjoying them-

selves present such a dismal and depressing spectacle
that all people not connected with these rich pleasure-
seekers appear by contrast to have all sorts of desirable
qualities.   Consequently I cannot trust myself to
write anything about the natives, with the exception
of the Balinese, with whom I did have some contact.
Also I am not in a position to say anything about the
Colonial policies pursued in these countries, except
to remark that to my mind the Dutch are over-
praised as colonisers ;   although they have been
relatively humane in recent years they have laid on
their subjects an overwhelming burden of crushing
and continuous taxation, which covers every part
of their lives ;   and since the revolt of the *Zieven
Provinzien* in 1931 the Dutch residents have been in a
continual state of panic.   The F.M.S. give the impression of being far more prosperous and better
developed ;   and Singapore is an interesting example
of the way mutually " hostile " groups can live
together in perfect amity when it is in the interest of
their governors that they should do so.   In the question
of conflicts between various groups or sects it is as
well to apply the maxim *cui bono*.

All that is necessary to say about the planters has
already been said by Mr. Somerset Maugham,
except that there are occasions when they take a rest
from murder and adultery and attend to their
plantations.   Incidentally that gentleman's name is a
Word of Power in the F.M.S. ;   to claim acquaintance
with him, or even to express admiration of his work

(I have only the right to the latter), will clear the space near you quicker than any other method I have ever heard of. Since every self-respecting person has read Mr. Maugham's stories I shall be able to call canoes canoes : the *prahus* and *dhows* are used by him far more skilfully than I could manage. I have no particular fondness for the " she sat upon her *dobi* " school of writing.

I am obviously debarred from writing a serious book about these regions ; and, indeed, they have been so thoroughly and learnedly discussed that it would need an exceptional traveller to add to the existing information in Dutch and French. Except on a few occasions, when I have quoted my sources, I have not hidden my own ignorance behind other people's knowledge. My chief interest in writing this book has been in trying to work out for myself the rôle of those illogical manifestations, art and religion, in the life of the community. For the benefit of those who desire a book to be useful, and a travel book to be helpful, I have given in an appendix the practical results of my journey.

July–November, 1935.

PART ONE

THE ROAD TO BALI

SUMATRA

As a generalisation I should say that I like scenery and dislike beauty spots. If I am forced to admire by notices or the consensus of public opinion I immediately become captious and fractious. The teutonic peoples, with their passion for never thinking for themselves when they can get anybody else to do so for them, plaster their mountains and lakes with notices leading to " höchst malerischer Aussichts-punkten," and boards to tell you when you have got there ; with the result that, as far as I am concerned, all the highly painterish view-places seem like particu-larly vulgar settings for Wagner's particularly vulgar operas. Were a German art-conscious municipality to be put in charge of Sumatra they would probably burst, as a chameleon is supposed to do on a tartan ; for there are only insignificant portions of this very large island which are not of almost overwhelming beauty. Fortunately it is in the hands of the Dutch who dislike scenery, having none at home ; all they do is to build excellent roads, and sigh when they look at hills which are still covered with uneconomic virgin forest instead of nice orderly plantations, or when they hear waterfalls, all of whose potential power is now wasted.

The Dutch appear to share with the French a dislike of untidy or exuberant nature ; Sumatra is one of the emptiest places with a tolerable climate in the world ; but you will hardly find a settler with as much ground round his house as would make a tennis-court. In this empty and fertile land the colonists build tiny bungalows of red tiles like council houses, so near to one another that you can smell when they are cooking onions three doors away ; in front of each house is a little strip of garden in which are cultivated with enormous difficulty asters and chrysanthemums and zinnias and phlox ; sometimes they will be so exotic as to grow cannas—though naturally only garden varieties—or geraniums ; the extraordinarily lovely flowers and ferns of the country are rigorously weeded out.

Since I left school I have never been an involuntary exile anywhere, so I cannot calculate the homesickness of those who unwillingly spend their lives in foreign countries ; the visible signs make it appear that the strain is overwhelming. There is something very pathetic about these dingy chrysanthemums grown with such care, while the wood opposite is dappled with orchids.

The life of a colonist must be very hard ; both you and your neighbours become so much larger than life. Besides the essential falsity of your position—so admirably analysed by George Orwell in his *Burmese*

Days—which poisons every activity, there is the horror of never being able for a moment to put on anonymity, to sink into the crowd. You can never do anything which everybody will not know ; you can never escape from your companions or yourself. Solitude is often tolerable ; in a crowd you are hidden and can, within irrational limits, choose your friends ; in a small and isolated community you have the worst of both conditions. Enforced companionship with a small group in whose composition you have had no say is probably the most unpleasant of all human conditions, the most nerve-racking, and the most destructive. Nowadays, with the improvements of transport, such small groups are becoming rare ; their chief survivals are in school-staffs, " old-fashioned " families, and among colonial administrators, merchants, and planters. And by no means all people in colonies are in this unhappy situation ; I should say about a hundred adults is the minimum group in which selection for compatibility can take place ; in groups of more than that number people can start to live in private again.

The Dutch are fortunate in not having developed a race-consciousness, or colour-bar ; they treat Europeans and Asiatics alike on a basis of economical and social distinctions. That is to say they are willing to associate with, and even on occasion to marry, rich and genteel Javanese ; they would no more think of associating with the common Asiatic than with the common European workman. In Java this gives quite an extension to social intercourse ; but in Sumatra there are no natives of a class one would leave cards on except in a couple of towns on the coast ; the natives are only suitable for servants, workers, or mistresses.

The Dutch officials and planters I came in contact with seemed to me to be far more educated than their opposite numbers in any other country. They nearly all of them spoke and read in five languages, and in most communities there are musical clubs. Most Dutch people also seem to have a passion for bridge.

The universal solace however among the Dutch in the colonies, as it seems to me to be among all European exiles (with the exception of the French in Indo-China, who have learned to smoke opium), is alcohol. I have already been publicly and privately reprimanded for saying that most Europeans in West Africa drink excessively, and I have gone to the trouble of enquiring from a couple of coasters who objected to this statement what they considered to be heavy drinking. They replied that they considered no man drunk who could put himself to bed. By that standard few people get drunk and that seldom ; I was talking about the amount of alcohol habitually consumed, irrespective of its effect on the drinker. Most people I have met who live in the tropics drink there a considerable amount and regularly. Nor is it surprising that they should do so. In their life they have no privacy, no companionship, no emotional contact—sexual relationships with natives are almost entirely prophylactic on one side and commercial on the other— ; if they have any intellectual or æsthetic interests it is improbable that they will be able to share them ; they can never act without reflection, for they have their prestige and dignity to consider ; nothing is left but drink.   With drink for a few hours they can think themselves happy, forget the tics and mannerisms of their companions which gnaw their nerves, forget their dignity and their fear.   For the great majority of people life in the tropics seems to me to be tragically unhappy ; they make money, but they cannot spend it ; life at home goes on without them so that when they return, whether on leave or to retire, they have neither contact nor place ; to live in the tropics is to go to prison—rather to be executed, so that you are capable of feeling pain, but only spurious pleasure, of hating, but not of loving. People cannot live properly in an alien climate among alien people, unless they are upheld by some high sustaining motive ;   and making money or safe-guarding property, whether for yourself or others, may be an inspiration, but it is such an ignoble one that those engaged in it have to invent high-sounding names to gull their own consciences.

I think it may be said as a generalisation that Orientals despise Europeans, even when they are afraid of them, thinking them ugly, and clumsy and gross and stupid : for Hindus and Mohammedans they are also infidels and unclean.   This attitude is on the whole unjustified ;   although Orientals have not yet made as much of a mess of their lives as we have, although they are not yet faced with apparently ineluctable death from starvation or poison gas, their escape is I think chiefly due to inertia. With the exception of the Balinese, Orientals are living on their past ; they made a lot of art and history some hundreds (in some cases thousands) of years ago, and are now engaged in exploiting it. When they have woken up they have shown that they can be just as greedy and brutal and short-sighted and murderous as their Occidental models. The Oriental seems far more alien to me than the African negro, for the very reason that the former are so like us ; except for rare isolated communities there seems to me to be little difference of quality, as opposed to degree, between people with whitish-pink and brownish-yellow skins. They are therefore to me—with the exception of these small communities—of very little interest ; unless, there are fundamental differences I am more interested in my compatriots. I do not think we have anything to learn from the Asiatics, except from the Chinese and Japanese good manners ; I also think there is very little we can teach them, except labour-saving devices.

There are a number of tribes in different stages of civilisation scattered over Sumatra, perhaps a dozen in all. The total population of the island is about eight million people, the average density of population being about forty-five to the square mile. We made a diagonal cut across the centre of the island and only stayed for any time among two of the tribes, the Batak and the Menangkabau. I heard however a good deal about the Achinese in the north of the island from various sources. They are still very imperfectly " civilised," or tamed ; all the men carry unsheathed knives with them when they walk abroad. I heard of two or three instances when they had ambushed and held up travellers and searched their baggage for arms. They still retain their original religion, in which the elephant plays a part as a sacred animal ; a little while ago a group of soldiers captured a young one and escorted it down to the coast, with the intention of shipping it to some European zoo ; the Achinese ambushed the party and let the god escape, risking their lives and liberty to prevent blasphemy. The country they inhabit is mostly low-lying, fever-haunted jungle.

The Batak inhabit the central highlands, from behind Medan to Lake Toba, rather thinly scattered in small communities ; the greater part of their land is useful and healthy for Europeans, though there are some barren stretches. Until the beginning of this century the Batak appear to have undergone very little outside influence. They were cannibals, and had evolved an individual and in some ways elaborate culture. They are a very peculiar physical type, with almost European features, their nose being far straighter and thinner than among Mongols, and their complexion appears to be sallow ; but all I saw were so dirty that it was impossible to guess the real colour of their skins. They are fairly short and squat, appear very unfriendly, and have nearly all a surly and suspicious expression. The women dress themselves in dark cloth of their own weaving, which covers them from neck to wrist and ankle ; and on their heads they lay a piece of cloth about four yards square, folded so that it balances like a big cushion. They are quite good metal workers and make for themselves elaborate silver ornaments, of which the most extraordinary are earrings about six inches across, shaped like the hook of a hook-and-eye, the broad portion facing backwards and serving as supports to the head-cloths. They also make large and well-worked rings and necklaces.

Their architecture is as fantastic as their costume. Near Brastagi most of the building is done with bamboos, and various dried and dyed leaves ; on Samosir with carved and dyed wood. The unit of domestic architecture is the family barn, or long house ; this is a rectangular building, any size up to sixty by thirty feet, raised about five feet off the ground on stilts ; the space underneath serves as a shelter for domestic animals. The floor is reached from the ground by a short ladder, which can be removed if necessary. Round the outside of the building runs a balcony, shaded by the eaves, on which most of the household tasks are done ; this is backed by about six foot of wall, pierced with a few doors ; above that the roofs begin. The Batak have an excessive interest in roofs ; it might be said, indeed,

Batak village near Brastagi, showing dwelling-house and storehouses

that their buildings consist of little else. They start as ordinary very steep thatched roofs, sloping gradually inwards ; in the simplest buildings this continues for about fifteen feet and then the thatching of the narrower ends is left off ; the wider sides are continued to make a ridge, and the narrower gable-ends filled in with an upright triangular piece of plaited withy, made into the most elaborate and ingenious coloured patterns and designs, sometimes representing people or animals, sometimes symmetrical arabesques, and in the village of Kabandjahé worked in strips of black and white so as to resemble Tudor half-timber. The gable-ends will be finished off with a carved animal's head, and in the centre of the roof is a peculiar little structure, also carved and coloured. Such air and light as the interior of the building receives comes through the plaited screens. This is the simplest type of building ; some, more elaborate, start a second roof over-jutting the first, and have odd inconsequential gables running out from the sides ; they are crowned by peculiar-looking pigeon lofts, which are themselves miniature houses. Besides the dwelling-houses there are also store-chambers and meeting-places, in which the architectural fantasy runs riot to produce buildings more eccentric than any European rococo. The roofs are " waisted," narrower in the middle than at the bottom or top ; the real building is surmounted by a scale model of itself, which is in turn surmounted by yet a tinier model ; and many other conceits.

On the island—or rather peninsula—of Samosir
in Lake Toba the buildings are smaller and are made
almost entirely of wood ; they are extremely beautifully decorated, the beam-ends being especially finely
carved. Some of the carvings are vaguely Chinese in
motive ; they are carved very shallowly, even when
they are in the round, as though the carvers had
learned to work on stone with inadequate tools. On
this island there are a number of carved stone
sarcophagi, very large and clumsy ; on the head is
seated a little manikin, with an over-sized head with
a flat head-dress, his knees drawn up to his chin and
his hands clasping them ; the top of the sarcophagus
is raised to a point, gradually rising higher than the
head of the manikin ; the flat side, facing away from
the block, is carved into a large face, rather majestic
and terrifying ; and squatting under this god-face
on the ground sits another little manikin, ithyphallic.

Besides their skill in building, weaving, and metal
working, the Batak had apparently evolved a form of
picture-writing ; in the Batak museum there are
pieces of bark covered with stylised signs, which have
no label attached to them, but which seem to me to
be indubitably communications.

Anthropologists, acting on the well-known principle
that everybody has come from somewhere else,
claim various parts of the Asiatic mainland as their
original home ; apparently there is some linguistic
connection with some tribe somewhere in British

India. Culturally there seem to be absolutely no connections. For anthropologists Sumatra was originally inhabited by Negritoes (who may have come from Australia), who were completely exterminated, so that no trace was left of them, by the pre-Malays.

Anthropologists resemble society hostesses in many ways—an anthropologist talking to a " savage " is just like a lady putting a " not quite quite " at her ease—and one of the most remarkable characteristics of both is this passion for placing people. As soon as an anthropologist hears about a new race, his first question is : " Who were their people ? What, pre-Malay ? They've got a place somewhere up in Cambodia, I believe. Of course, the Khmers took the family place, and they had to move ; and they replaced some people who were quite outside the pale, in fact extinct." I have not sufficient knowledge to be able to assert that some people are still living in their land of origin ; I can't see however why they shouldn't be.

As far as I can understand the views of the Diffusionists they consider that any human invention is made only once by one man in one place. Some years ago somebody in the valley of the Nile (or the Indus) suddenly said : " I say, you chaps, why don't we build houses instead of living in caves ? " or " Don't you think religion would be rather a good idea ? " This suggestion was at once adopted and missionary parties sent out to tell the rest of the world, who had up to then been making artificial caves if they couldn't find real ones, and not wondering about how things happened at all. Of course, things might have happened like that in those high and far-off times ; but I should suggest that nobody should be allowed to make theories about the past or the exotic until they had produced some moderately sensible obser- vations on the behaviour of the people in the next street. When people can't check up on you it's too easy to appear wise.[1]

Wherever the Batak did come from they had been complete masters of their part of the country from their arrival until almost the beginning of this century. It was only the invention of the motor and the boom in rubber which made the centre of Sumatra worth colonising. The Batak had to be won over, or at any rate tamed, for the earlier method of colonisation, by which one merely killed the original inhabitants, was now seen to be wasteful and short-sighted ; to achieve this, the Dutch imported boatloads of mission- aries. The missionaries quickly persuaded the Batak that dogs were quite as good eating as their fellows ; they wooed them with honeyed words and dotted the countryside with horrid little corrugated iron

[1] I am indebted to my friend Professor Lancelot Hogben for the best anti-diffusionist illustration I know of. In 1690 Takebe in Japan gave the value of pi as an unlimited series with a value correct to fifty decimal places in our notation. This was first worked out in Europe by Gregory and Wallis in 1660. There seems absolutely no possibility of there having been any com- munication between Japan and England on the subject.

chapels. Apparently the Batak respond extremely well to European education and become very capable underlings ; even in their uneducated state they are extraordinarily good chess-players. In their villages they are as unappetising-looking a crowd as can well be imagined, dirty and disease-ridden and scowling.

Most of their land is six thousand feet or more above sea level. It is very variegated country. Round Brastagi the steep hills corroded with waterfalls are covered with the virgin forest of an indescribably tender green ; under the big trees, smothered with parasites and lianas, grow the most exotic and lovely varieties of palm and banana and tree-fern ; the ground is covered with small flowers such as *impatiens* and a plant like balsam ; the blue *ipomæa* and the passion-flower cover the low-lying bushes ; white and brown orchids (the white are *Miltonia*, but I cannot identify the brown) hang high in the air, and a purple orchid-like plant grows in the grass. Through gaps in the trees you can see down to the Indian Ocean, six thousand feet below and thirty miles away ; while dominating the landscape is the volcano Sibajak, its open sulphurous crater showing on the pink rock like a suppurating boil. As you go further inland the country becomes arid, and you cross bracken-covered heaths which in temperature and vegetation recall Dartmoor in the spring ; then descend again to the huge inland Toba Lake, almost cobalt blue, with steep grassy hills running

down to it in spurs, for all the world like the Nor-
wegian fjords. From there the ground descends
precipitately by a nerve-racking road with uncount-
able hairpin bends, till you come to Sibolga and the
West Coast, the laughing sea dotted with tiny
palm-covered islands, picturesque beyond reality.

Compared with the Batak, the Manengkabau are
extremely respectable, so respectable in fact that
some anthropologists have made them the starting
place for the Malay race and language. (That
doesn't prevent them having come from somewhere
else too ; in fact they must have, for otherwise how
did they get there ?) Also they are Mohammedans, and
therefore in no need of missionary efforts ; they make
their own bromides. They seem superficially a
dull people, less interesting than the Batak, though
more friendly, and if not handsome, at least tolerable
looking ; they weave very pretty materials with silk
and metal threads, and make excruciating and
tortured silver-wire work ; their buildings, though
not extravagant after the Batak fashion, are fairly odd.
They too are rectangular buildings on stilts ; but
the walls behind the balconies are higher, and are
quite prettily decorated with coloured patterned
panels, generally red and blue. The thatched roofs

rise less steeply and are slightly concave, and the top ridge is on a curve, the ends being considerably higher than the middle. The middle third of this ridge has an additional roof identical in shape with the bigger one ; it occasionally serves a structural purpose by covering a small attic, but is usually purely ornamental ; the Manengkabau building presents a skyline of four wedge-like gables in a row, curved on the inside and cut away on the outside, this appearance being known to the natives as the she-elephant-on-her-back. These buildings are quite pretty when thatched ; but such can only be found in out-of-the-way communities ; the Manengkabau are civilised, and consequently their buildings, from mosques to storehouses, are roofed with corrugated iron.

The only two concrete gifts (as opposed to hygiene and education) that Europe has given to non-European civilisations are corrugated iron and artificial illumination. It is hard to decide which of the two have been the more valuable. Corrugated iron is undoubtedly the ugliest building material in the world, but it is cheap, easy to employ, and keeps out the damp (though it concentrates the heat). The benefits of powerful artificial light in the tropics, which only have twelve hours of daylight, are incalculable. I can think of no other European invention or device which has really been of use to non-Europeans. I have not heard of a race which has not produced satisfactory clothing for itself, usually far better than what they now buy ; they have nearly all discovered sufficient agriculture for their needs, and, at any rate in rice-eating countries, evolved an adequate system of irrigation. All of the larger Oriental countries had a literate class long before we did. Europe could give non-Europeans more leisure through labour-saving devices, a longer expectation of life through medical services, and a more complete diet by imports and teaching them large-scale agriculture for their own use. Actually they have to work harder than ever before as coolies to pay their taxes ; although infantile mortality has gone down somewhat, the average expectation of life in British India is, I believe, twenty-three (as opposed to sixty in England) ; and most colonial peoples are under-nourished and badly nourished since they have no time to attend to their own agriculture (or, if they do, have to sell so much of their produce to pay taxes) and have to live on imported or ready prepared food.

I am quite unable to evolve a theoretical colonial policy which can satisfy me ethically. To what extent tropical produce is essential to-day for the maintenance of the standard of life in temperate countries is a very disputable question. If cellulose, electricity, and alcohol were exploited to the extent of which they are capable there would be little need for cotton, coal, or petrol. It is almost certain that with sufficient inducements botanists could produce varieties of tobacco and tea which would be hardy in temperate climates. Rice is already grown in Southern Europe. With the possible exception of

Manengkabau house in the Padang Highlands:
" The she-elephant-on-her-back "
In front is a storehouse for rice

coffee and cocoa, the tropics produce few important materials which we could not produce ourselves, did not powerful interests and easy profits block the way. Meanwhile I do not desire to forgo the gains to European life of tropical agriculture—I do not desire to forgo the gains of any system, only to remove their undesirable qualities—but I cannot see how they are to be obtained at present without condemning large portions of mankind to a very unpleasant life. To withdraw from the colonies or to give them " home rule " is no solution. To put the colonies at the mercy of some other exploiter is pure Pontius-Pilatism ; and they have been so corrupted by European influence that home rule would merely mean that the people would exchange greedy European taskmasters for greedier taskmasters of their own colour. The conditions in Indian-owned cotton mills are no argument for native control. I do not share the view of the Labour Party that everything is all right provided people can vote ; and I rebel at the fatalism of the Communists who consider that every nation has to go through the same purgatory of exploitation to produce a class-conscious proletariat, the only means of salvation. I cannot see why salvation, as well as exploitation, should not be imposed from above.

According to Dutch informants, the Manengkabau have acquired so much civilisation that they are now resisting exploitation. Fort de Kock, their principal town, was described to me as a hotbed of Communism. What that means it is of course quite impossible

c

to say ; it might possibly mean Communism, though the full attendance at the mosques makes me doubt it ; it probably means grumbling and possibly sporadic strikes. East of Suez any murmur other than a prayer and any movement other than a salaam is a sign of Communism. It seems to me a pity that no Empire-builder is ever allowed to know what Communism is ; even if their lives are to be devoted to combating it, it would be as well if they knew what they were fighting, and did not confuse any sign of disaffection or discontent, mostly of an anarchical nature, with the strivings for a planned and possibly over-logical order. And if their aim is to destroy Communism, they almost certainly overreach their object in so describing any activity they dislike ; if people who have merely tried to right what they consider intolerable conditions are treated as Communists, they may try to find out what that label means.

The more intelligent Dutchmen I talked to are far more frightened of Japan than of the Soviets, and not unreasonably ; and the pro-Japanese policy of Great Britain fills them, as it fills every realistically minded person south and east of Singapore, with the greatest apprehension. The unofficial Holy Alliance with Germany and Japan against Russia is making England suspect, not only in the greater part of Europe, but also in the whole of the Pacific. From the point of view of peace and also for the preservation of the Empire—if these objects are considered desirable—the greed and desire for revenge on the part of a few people in this country should be forcibly restrained. Probably nobody now imagines that Russia has any aggressive intentions ; she is only dangerous as an example if conditions outside her boundaries are worse than inside. Active and expensive preparations for war undoubtedly worsen these conditions ; and the miseries and privations which the most successful war would produce would almost certainly lead to some form of Communism in the belligerent countries, even if it were (which seems to me an impossibility) stamped out in Russia. People who are frightened of Communism should devote every penny they can to improving the lot of their compatriots and subjects ; anti-Communism merely shows people the way there. Meanwhile the people who have supported Japan and Germany would do well to listen to the conversations of educated Dutchmen and New Zealanders and Australians. If politicians are ever capable of learning anything, it would be extremely instructive for them.[1]

Although the Manengkabau are now all Moham-medans they have preserved some relics of the Buddhistic Hinduism which preceded Islam. The chief of these is a vague belief in transmigration ; there are sacred fishponds, whose inhabitants—a sort of carp —house the souls of ancestors ; it is a meritorious act to feed these fishes ; and when they die their bodies

[1] Tea-planters particularly resent the anti-Russian policy of the British Government, which closes to them a potentially enormous market for their at present unsaleable produce.

are wrapped in pieces of cloth and buried with appropriate rites. There are also a few monuments left ; but they can only interest professional archæologists.

The country in which they live—the Padang highlands—has quite a different character to the Batak country, as though nature changed south of the ·Equator. The landscape is far more violent, with precipitous mountains, deep and sudden cañons, unexpected lakes. The vegetation too is far richer in colouring, nearer the emerald than Brastagi, though equally varied. The constant but everchanging beauty of the landscape is fatiguing, for there is hardly a mile anywhere which can be neglected ; it is a series of high spots without intervening " flats," when the senses can rest. The most magnificent drive of the lot is from Fort de Kock to Padang Pandjang, past Lake Singarak, over the wind-swept highlands to Alahan Pandjang, and then down to the sea through the Soebang Pass. In half a day you pass through every type of scenery that nature can offer (except snow-mountains)—heaths, lakes, cultivated land, the forest, the jungle, and the sea. As you descend the pass the virgin forest on either side of the road goes through every combination of vegetation from pines to palms, tree ferns and more exotic plants. Nowhere in the world that I know has nature been so prodigal.

THE ROAD TO BALI

JAVA

Java MAKES its chief appeal to the professional
botanist. The botanical gardens at Buitenzorg
constitute the finest tropical arboretum in the world—
they are also very pleasant to wander through—and
the application of scientific research on plant genetics
and ecology practised in the various plantations makes
them of the greatest interest to the scientist, and an
object-lesson and a standing shame to all other
colonial powers. From nearly every crop the Dutch
gain a vastly greater proportional yield than any other
nation.

The Englishman's dislike of science is one of the
major mysteries of the English character. As a nation
we loathe and distrust scientists. We do everything
we can to prevent people engaging in scientific
research ; no man of ability can hope to earn by
research a tenth of what he can gain more easily in
the service of some firm ; and we permit and even
encourage anti-vivisectionists, who for obscurantism
and harm are far more pernicious than fundamentalists.
Even if they could prove that scientists ever inflicted

unavoidable pain on animals for pleasure,[1] they would not by entirely abolishing vivisection diminish animal suffering so much as they would by stopping the preserving and shooting of game. For the health and well-being of the country anti-vivisection pamphlets should be treated in exactly the same way as seditious pamphlets ; anti-scientific agitation should be treated as treason ; and the bother and expense of obtaining licences to kill animals should be transferred, without alteration, to sportsmen.

If the cost of a single battleship were devoted to the erection of proper buildings, and the price of its yearly maintenance devoted to paying competent men the same salary as they can now only get for working on scents or beer, there is no reason why we should not equal and surpass Dutch attainments in botany, instead of, as now, being shamed by them.

For those, like myself, whose knowledge of scientific botany is negligible, Java offers few attractions other than volcanoes. For the Dutch tourist agencies the one thing foreigners really like is volcanoes ; and in Java you can walk up to them, drive up to them, ride up to them, or fly over them. Since this inducement is so widely offered there must be some demand for it ; but except for excessively Freudian reasons I cannot understand it ; as far as I am concerned one volcano is as boring as the next one.

[1] If there are people who cannot be happy unless they are actively cruel I am sufficiently patriotic to prefer that animals, rather than men, should be their victims. If Goering wasn't so fond of animals. . . .

The Borobodur from the top terrace, showing part
of the central stûpa, and the smaller hollow stûpas,
each containing a Buddha

*The surrounding bell has been removed from the
Buddha in the foreground*

Round the volcanoes small beauty-spots have been preserved, one or two of them, such as Kawah Kamodjan and the Dieng plateau, quite pleasant; otherwise as much as I saw of it Java's scenery is dull and monotonous. The country is so thickly populated that there are very few stretches without corrugated iron roofs, and the model cultivation is æsthetically uninteresting. Rice terraces give character to a landscape, but tea plantations look like a Victorian laurel shrubbery, extending over miles; the teak is an ugly tree with its big bilious leaves, and it is planted in geometrical forests; the young rubber trees have spindly trunks and dirty leaves. In Java as a whole there is no fresh colour.

There are four towns in Java which would be considered important in any European country; but it would be difficult to find in Europe four towns of as little interest. The old quarter of Batavia, with its canals and its red brick houses, has the picturesque qualities of the old and shabby; the ethnological museum there is not entirely uninteresting and there is a small aquarium in Batavia and a small zoo in Sourabaya which contain a few uncommon animals and fishes, including in Sourabaya adult gorillas. Otherwise these towns have as little interest, character, or beauty as Zenith, where Mijnheer Babbitt sells real estate. There are, it is true, slums full of Javanese and Chinese as there is probably a negro quarter in Zenith; the climate and the bright clothes worn by the inhabitants prevent these parts being wholly depressing. But to get any pleasure out of such a spectacle you must consider people with a deeper pigmentation to be of another species to yourself, untouched by poverty and discomforts and squalor.

The Javanese are, I am told, a fairly homogeneous Malay people ; they seem, however, to change in character as one goes eastward, becoming progressively more and more dour and drab. There are a number of small tribes with slight linguistic and cultural differences of behaviour in the interior. They are all Mohammedans.

I did not personally find the Javanese very sympathetic ; despite their fertility they give somehow the impression of being a race of old and exhausted people, only half alive. This impression may I think be due partly to their religion, and to the abysmal poverty of the greater number. Poverty, especially uncomplaining and involuntary poverty, is numbing and repulsive anywhere ; and Mohammedanism is the most deadening of all creeds. A purely personal point which prevented me enjoying their company was the question of size ; I do not like being among people who appear smaller and weaker than I am, unless they have corresponding superiority elsewhere ; I dislike the company of those I feel to be my inferiors. In very early youth the Javanese boys are pretty and the girls sometimes very handsome and attractive ; but such beauty is very transient. The poverty and unemployment has caused a great deal of prostitution

on the part of both sexes ; in the towns the more
enterprising pursue you on bicycles.

Javanese art is a galvanised corpse. Such as it is,
it is a relic of pre-Mohammedan Hinduism. It
consists of performances of episodes from the Ramayana
in a variety of media, through living actors, puppets,
and shadows thrown on a screen. Except that in the
last two cases the dialogue is recited by a single person
there is little difference between the performances.
They are all spoken in High Javanese, a language not
one ordinary person in fifty properly understands ;
they are all stylised out of all relation with life ; and
the musical accompaniment seems to me to be without
interest or invention.

The stylisation of movement for the actors requires
very elaborate training, and has produced a few
interesting poses and movements. The most novel
of these is the stance for male dancers with the feet
some way apart and pointing at right angles to the
body ; the knees are bent and the thighs are opened
so that they lie in the same plane as the trunk ; the
arms are also held akimbo in the same plane, so that
the man becomes an almost flat and excessively
angular creature ; this is as it were position one for
male dancers, and most of the dancing is elaborations
from this position. It is effective for some dramatic
dancing, particularly fighting dances. Whereas the
men exaggerate their bones and angles, women
pretend they have none ; women dancers approximate
as nearly as they can to an upright snake or eel, or a

boneless wonder. To enhance this effect they are hung about with pieces of soft drapery, and hold another length of material in their left hand, which they twitch rhythmically. The costumes worn by the actors are rather pretty; the men wear knee-length tight breeches, and over that a skirt split at the sides in a contrasting material, so arranged that a tail falls in front, the legs being unhampered by the low drapery; this skirt is held in place by a broad belt about half-way between the navel and the breasts; except for ornaments, the top of the body is bare. They wear extraordinarily elaborate head-dresses of thin worked metal, whose protuberances indicate the rôle and rank of the player. Demons wear fantastic masks, and gods open-work wings attached to the shoulder and hip; human beings wear an exaggeratedly martial make-up of a deep red-brown, with heavy black eyebrows and moustaches. Women have a pale ochre make-up; their dresses are usually fastened directly under the arms and fall to the ground; they often are made of as many as seven different materials. They too wear elaborate head-dresses. The hero usually has as companion a clown with no head-dress and a white make-up, who supplies the comic relief and speaks understandably; his is the only part of the perform-ance really appreciated by the majority of the audience. It is rather as if performances of Greek tragedy, done in the Bradfield manner, were the only available entertainment, made tolerable by the insertion of a part for George Robey.

Detail of a panel in the Borobodur

The puppet plays and shadow plays are even less interesting ; the only pleasure to be derived from them being the ingenuity with which the dolls and silhouettes are manipulated. The dolls have, besides the usual hold, as in Punch and Judy shows, thin sticks attached to their wrists, so that the arms can be moved realistically ; they have nearly as much life in their movements as the dancers. The silhouette figures, cut out of leather, have a certain weak rococo elegance. They are thrown on to a linen screen, lit from behind. There are some amusing stylisations of scenery in these performances, a pointed fan representing a mountain, and so on.

Occasionally by the wayside slightly more amusing entertainments can be found ; we came upon quite a pleasant bamboo orchestra, and somewhere near Pekalongan half a dozen youths, dressed in short sarongs and wearing krisses, were doing a stylised and hieratic dance to celebrate the gathering of the first rice ; an older man had two baskets of rice slung on a pole over his shoulder, and a notice hanging from the pole explaining the ceremony ; he beat time with rattles. At Bandoeng the Chinese were celebrating their New Year with a five days' fair ; besides the ordinary attractions of side-shows and darts, there were gambling tents, where for a few days the Oriental could legitimately indulge his strongest passion—the Dutch forbid gambling ordinarily under very severe penalties ; if people lose their money, how are they to pay taxes ?—; cloth dragons on four human legs

with huge heads covered with tassels ran about the
crowd and into the different houses, stamping on
the fire crackers which were thrown to them ; the
" classics " were performed in an improvised theatre,
while outside people in masks indulged in indecorous
pantomimes, and jugglers performed the nauseating
trick of putting people into trance and removing
(or appearing to remove) their entrails, waving them
at the crowd, then replacing them, sewing up and
resuscitating the victim.   I can think of ways how this
could be faked.

At Djocjakarta there was a " modern " theatre,
where under the old conventions modern plays,
inspired by the more naïve films, were performed.
I have never seen anywhere such dull and apathetic
playing, not even in the West End of London.   Boys
took the women's rôles.

Djocjakarta and its neighbourhood is the only
portion of Java which to my mind repays the
journey.   Its chief interest, of course, lies in the ruins
of the different Hindu and Buddhist temples ; all
the most important are within fifty miles of this town.
Moreover, at Djocjakarta and Soerakarta the work
of colonisation has been carried out slightly less
thoroughly than elsewhere ; the old sultanates still
remain with their full ceremonial and protocol, even
though the powers of the sultans are extremely limited.

We received a printed permit to visit the kraton, or
royal establishment, of Soerakarta.   On this permit
were printed a number of rules in three languages.

It was forbidden to take photographs or notes in the kraton, to pass any remark about it or any feature of it in any language, to measure, or attempt to compute, or enquire as to its size, the number of its inhabitants, or any other detail, whether of the whole or a part. Visitors must dress as though they were visiting a European sovereign.

We were very uncomfortably hot in our dark clothes when we arrived at the entrance at the indicated hour. Once there we had to get our permit signed and countersigned ; pass through a series of sentries, and then wait till an escort should arrive. We were shown over the buildings by one of the sultan's descendants, a youthful prince who was, without exception, the most beautiful person I have ever seen, languid and graceful as a Persian miniature. His complexion was the warm brown of some Spaniards, a trifle red on the cheeks, his slightly pouting lips almost crimson ; his features were extremely regular, and his large dark eyes a perfect almond, fringed with incredibly long, curved lashes. His black hair grew low and irregular. He was very short and slight, but perfectly proportioned ; like all the other male inhabitants of the kraton he had his breasts and arms bare ; he was dressed in a sarong of brown batik, with a broad waistband of green velvet, which surrounded his body several times ; in the band were fixed two krisses, one with a plain wooden handle, upright against his spine, the golden wood only a little lighter in texture than the skin it touched ; the other, slung at his side, was handsome with silver and diamonds. He was very friendly, with an easy smile, and I should think as intelligent as a well-trained dog ; what need has such a perfect animal of more ?

The kraton is a complete self-contained town, any and every trade and occupation being pursued within its walls. It would make an admirable place to study native handicraft of every sort ; the husking, kneading and milling of grain, the spinning, weaving, dyeing, and painting of batik, the carving and working of wood, the illumination of manuscripts. The library contained some very fine hand-painted books ; and copies were being made and new records compiled by grave-faced clerks in spectacles ; all the older men wore their hair long and twisted into a bun at the nape of the neck, in the Singhalese fashion. There were a number of soldiers and guardians about the building, dressed like janisseries in a comic opera, with hats like black japanned flower pots, immensely brawny shoulders, and huge, broad swords flapping at their sides.

Much of what we were shown was of little interest— unwieldy state carriages, collections of fairly modern arms, and so on; there was however an extremely fine collection of old masks and puppets and shadow-play fans, some of them very lovely. Naturally we did not see the private apartments of the Sultan, but only the state rooms. The most important of these was the dancing-room, an immense raised marble floor with a low ceiling supported by numberless columns ;

The Buddha in the Mendoet Temple

the other state rooms were of a similar design, but were rendered hideous by bad modern marble life-size statues, man-high bronze candelabra fitted with electricity, and enormous crystal chandeliers.

Our visit coincided with the Sultan's return from a visit to Sumatra ; to celebrate this happy event the dancers gave a morning performance to their returning lord. The orchestra was in an adjoining room, but separated from the dancing chamber by a partition of wood and glass ; the music was relayed electrically. We were given seats in the shadow of one corner, standing up when the Sultan appeared, dim and grotesque and enormous, and took up his place on the throne on the opposite side. The music started and a crowd of women dressed in brown and yellow crawled on their hands and knees past the Sultan over the dancing floor and took up their positions, one between every four columns. Except when dancing no one stands erect before Majesty. The individual dancers were not particularly interesting, swaying and writhing, barely taking their feet off the floor ; the effect of the whole was enchanting. The colonnades were so long that the far perspectives were sensibly diminished ; the marble floor reflected like a cloudy mirror ; as far as eye could see the same movements of bodies and draperies were echoed and reflected endlessly, as unreal as a scene from the *Arabian Nights*. We were not, unfortunately, allowed to see the boy dancers who followed.

The kraton of Djocjakarta is a poor copy of

Soerakarta, with little to interest. There is however an abandoned palace there, the Water Castle, which has enormous baroque charm. It is a straggling series of buildings, mostly of dull red brick, interspersed with gardens and courtyards and ponds ; the royal living-rooms were underground and flooded, beds and canopies floating on running water. The place is made almost intolerable by the persistence of batik-sellers, whom nothing can discourage. Most of the modern batik strikes me as very ugly, of no more interest than European printed cottons with all-over patterns in two or three drab colours (mostly brown or blue) on a white ground ; some of the old silk batik is quite elegant, but the native-woven materials of the Menangkabau, the Batak, and the Cambodians are far pleasanter and more vivid ; those of Bali of the greatest beauty and splendour.

The object of the greatest single interest in Java is the ruined Buddhist stûpa, or memorial shrine, the Borobodur. People even claim that it is the finest of all Indian buildings. Since I have not yet been to India I cannot tell whether this is true or not, but I sincerely hope not, for as a piece of architecture it is only equalled in insignificance and lack of interest by the Pyramids, and as a shape it is even uglier. It is a squat square pyramid, built round a hillock ; each side has a double projection, that is to say that if each side were divided into six equal parts the second and fifth project over the first and sixth, and the third and fourth over the second and fifth. By

Vishnu as a Bull
An idol in the Prambanan Temples

this means the building appears from a little distance
to be circular, and at the top the square is circled.
The building consists of a series of galleries or terraces ;
above the base are four galleries of decreasing height
sculptured on both sides, then three circular terraces
dotted with small stûpas, shaped like open-work bells
with long handles, or cloches, a Buddha inside each
lattice-work of stone ; in the centre is the real shrine,
a gigantic solid stûpa or stone bell, surmounted by a
huge octagonal column which was originally crowned
with three stone umbrellas. The sides of the
building also are covered with numberless Buddhas,
each in a pinnacled niche ; the whole effect is
like a slightly squashed bowler-hat, bristling with
spikes.

This symmetrical mess of stone is covered with the
most lovely sculpture. Except for the numberless
Buddhas, seated with folded legs and with the hands
and arms in the (I think) ninety-two hieratic positions,
and a few heraldic beasts by the doorways, it is all
in low relief, mostly on sandstone, much worn by
corrosion and exposure and difficult to see except in
the right light. Round the four galleries, a long
pilgrimage, the story of the Buddha in his different
incarnations and that of the different Bodhisattvas are
carved. The stories are often difficult to follow, but
the grace, composition, and liveliness of the different
panels—for it is all panelled—need no interpretation.
A number of different sculptors, of varying merit and
with different visions, were employed in this work ;

D

and the repeated compositions and mannerisms in
panels often far apart let one think that the work of
different artists can be identified. The frieze of the
Parthenon has more gallantry and gaiety, a more
immediate appeal ; parts of the friezes of Borobodur
are, to my taste, equally satisfying. Their position,
on either side of narrow galleries, makes them almost
impossible to photograph.

Hard by the Borobodur is a small rectangular
shrine, the Mendoet temple. Its exterior, save for a
handsome stairway, is unenterprising ; the dark
interior contains the most beautiful Buddha I know,
one of the dozen or so masterpieces of sculpture in the
world. The Buddha is seated on a throne, over which
a drapery falls. He is naked except for a loin-cloth
which falls between his legs. He is portrayed as a
large and muscular, not particularly beautiful man.
His feet are together, his knees separated ; the elbows
are a little above and further out than the knees, the
fingers joined in the attitude of teaching. The noble
and contemplative head, with the eyes lowered, is
covered with symmetrical and stylised curls, and the
long ears are the only perpendicular lines in the
statue. Behind the head a curved and pointed fan
echoes and reverses the composition of the body, and
the back of the throne, spreading like wings from the
Buddha's shoulder, repeats on another plane the
parallels of the base. I know of no other single piece
of sculpture which so successfully combines every
canon of composition into a whole of such complicated

simplicity, so alive with dignity and holiness. Had I to choose an idol to pray to, this would be it.

To the east of Djocjakarta there are a number of small Hindu temples in various stages of decrepitude and restoration. Some of them have pleasantly decorated windows and doors, and pretty figures in the niches. One has life-size, slightly grotesque figures carved in relief from the blocks of limestone in the walls, the stones being hollowed out around the figures. The Prambanan temples, a group of about eight shrines, are more elaborate, with some pleasant reliefs, and half a dozen solid statues of the various Hindu divinities. I have seen too few of these many-headed and -handed grotesques to be able to judge of their merits ; the carving which pleased me best was one of Vishnu in his incarnation as a humped bull, a very lively and well-executed piece of observation.

BALI, OR LIFE AND RELIGION

BALI IS a small and mountainous island lying to the west of Java. It has an area of about two thousand square miles, and about a million inhabitants. It can almost be described as the end of the Western world, for there is as much difference between the birds and quadrupeds on it and on its neighbour Lombok (though they are separated only by a strait of fifteen miles) as there is between the fauna of England and Japan.[1] In the last ten years this island has been written about, filmed, photographed, and gushed over to an extent which would justify nausea. I went there half-unwillingly, for I expected an uninteresting piece of bali-hoo, picturesque and faked to a Hollywood standard; I left wholly unwillingly, convinced that I had seen the nearest approach to Utopia that I am ever likely to see.

Anthropologists call the Balinese an Indonesian people, and say that they came from South-East Asia; they allow this to have happened several thousand years ago. Starting from about the beginning of the Christian era, if not earlier, Bali was visited by Hindus; they must have conquered the

[1] See Wallace, *Island Life*, p. 4.

original inhabitants, for the ruling aristocracy are, and have been during the whole period for which written records remain—roughly a thousand years—Brahminic Hindus. But a person is born a Brahmin, nor can he become one by conversion, and therefore these Brahmins must almost certainly have Hindu descent in one line of their ancestry. Between roughly the years A.D. 800–1200 there was a great deal of connection between Bali and Java ; at one time they were incorporated in the same kingdom ; King Erlangga (991–1050), famous in poetry and myth, was a Balinese who ruled over the two islands. After Java's conversion to Mohammedanism the two countries seem to have had little intercourse with one another ; the few Balinese converts to Islam have always been regarded as social outcasts, and it is generally some crime involving ostracism which is the cause of conversion. It is almost certain that in present-day Balinese art and ritual we have a highly individualised version of the arts of Hindu Java as they existed before the drying wind of Allah blasted them. In this connection it is worth quoting the judgment of Dr. Stutterheim, one of the greatest living authorities on the antiquities of the Dutch East Indies. " With regard to (the difference in character between the two races)," he writes, " we must observe that the Balinese, in contrast with the Javanese . . . have a strong predilection for the baroque and for redundancy. While the Javanese, as a person, conveys the impression of modesty and reserve, the

Balinese asserts himself directly and is not averse to showing off. And while the Javanese in his demeanour is either a prince or slave, the Balinese has more of the self-confident free citizen ; on the whole there is more frankness in his disposition than in the nature of the Javanese ; he will not easily bear an injustice and will clearly give expression either to his approval or his disapproval. In contrast with the Javanese, who is bent on mysticism and relishes above all a profound discourse, the Balinese has a preference for things concrete. . . . The ideal of the Javanese is the refined knight, who bears misfortune and even injustice without flinching, but who also, in joy or triumph, is master of his emotions. He seeks the refined, even the subtle and spiritual, and his arts are marked by reserve and finesse. The Balinese, on the other hand, likes the more coarsely expressive in jest and earnest ; he is lavish with gilt and bright colours ; his music, though rich and melodious, is characteristically explosive. . . ."

This judgment by a learned man who has a year of experience for my every day, is worthy of consideration ; if you alter the implied bias my judgment would concur in almost every detail. I dislike princes and slaves equally ; the greatest charm of the Balinese is for me that they treat you as equal. I have no great love for the over-refined and meticulous (or anæmic) in art ; and I think Dr. Stutterheim is definitely unfair to Balinese achievements in music and the plastic arts.

From the fourteenth to the nineteenth centuries the Balinese lived fairly undisturbed, receiving occasional visits from European navigators. The real source of Balinese life was then, as it seems always to have been, the village community ; imposed from above, but barely amalgamating, were a group of princelets and lordlings, with varying spheres of influence and revenue. From the middle of the nineteenth century the Dutch settled on the north coast of the island ; and in 1906 obtained complete control of the island by one of the ugliest actions in the whole history of colonial exploitation. After six years of " pacification " the Balinese accepted the situation ; and the Dutch established the regime which is now in force. Once the fact of colonisation is admitted the way the Dutch have treated the island is highly commendable ; they have respected the desire of the Balinese to stay in their own country and not to have foreigners among them ; beyond abolishing widow-burning (sati is said to have existed before their arrival) and making cock-fighting and gambling illegal except on a few occasions, they have interfered very little with the habits of the inhabitants. Their preoccupation with tax-collection—the chief object and aim of colonisation—has had one very unfortunate result ; under the princes the best dancers, actors, and artists were given complete immunity from taxes ; the Dutch have refused to continue this (surely not very expensive) recognition of the arts, with the result that the drama particularly has fallen off very much. The

Dutch have very sensibly made it extremely difficult for people who have no business there to settle on the island, saving it from the fate of Hawaii and Tahiti ; and when I was there (February, 1935), they had so far resisted the importunity of Lutherans to allow them to send missionaries to the island. Another visitor, who was there after I was, hinted that the missionaries have now got their way ; but teasingly she would not be precise ; she too intends writing a book on the island.

If this is true it is a disaster of the greatest magnitude; even if Low-Church protestantism had anything to teach the Balinese, even if it were the greatest of all revelations, its introduction would inevitably destroy the unity and homogeneity which now make of Bali an object-lesson for the world. Actually I believe the missionaries to be almost wholly actuated by that itch to destroy all beauty and happiness which is alien to them, that canker of envy and spite which we call the Nonconformist conscience. For the Nonconformist conscience beauty and happiness are sin and obscenity ; incapable of either itself, it tries to destroy them for all others ; it is murderous and greedy, allowing all that is unpleasant and ugly, from its own services and chapels to the most inhuman methods of getting money ; it is ever prying into the enjoyments of its neighbours and seeking to destroy them, besmirching and defiling everything which is not included in its own mean creed. It is the supreme blasphemy, the curse which has turned

Tombs of the Kings in the
rocks at Gunoong Kawi
One of the oldest monuments in Bali

England (and to a great extent America) into the most hag-ridden and almost the ugliest country (architecturally) in the world. For the Nonconformist conscience is far more occupied with its neighbours' than with its own conduct.

The methods by which the missionaries tried to gain the Governor-General's permission to corrupt Bali are typical. The Balinese village is neat and orderly, but the roads are of earth, and after heavy tropical rain naturally look filthy. The missionaries took films of them in this condition, if necessary adding garbage of their own ; they hired the poorest and most diseased people they could find to parade in these puddled streets, and exhibited in Europe these artificially sordid pictures as typical of Balinese life ; and so worked on the feelings of the pious and humane to send monster petitions to the Governor-General, begging that the misery of such savages should be lightened by the good offices of the Lutheran Church. Hardly a week goes by, I am told, without the Governor receiving such an address. The means are worthy of the end. Those who, for whatever motive—be it humane, æsthetic, or sociological—consider this undesirable, would accomplish a useful action by sending protests against such activities to H.E. the Governor-General at Buitenzorg, Java.

If the population were distributed evenly over the island the average density would work out at something like 450 to the square mile. It is however much higher in the inhabited portions, for there are large tracts of land which will only support a very sparse population or none at all. Such are the east end of the island, mostly hilly scrub, and the higher parts of the central mountains, with peaks of from six to ten thousand feet. Consequently the sea-board and the lower slopes of the hills are covered with dwellings, and nearly every available yard of ground is cultivated.

The chief food—and also the chief export—of the Balinese is rice, and the countryside is covered with sawas, or rice terraces. The climate is so kind and uniform—there is never a rainless season, though the rains are less frequent in the summer months—and the volcanic soil so fertile that a crop of rice can be raised in four months, and each piece of land give two crops a year, after allowing for resting periods. Owing to these conditions the Balinese landscape has a peculiarly chequered appearance, for one terrace may have the rice ripe and golden, while its neighbours may be in their fresh green, or entirely flooded, or with the spikes of the young plants dappling the water, or even showing the bare red earth. With bamboo conduits the Balinese have worked out a system of irrigation on which Europeans have been unable to improve ; the irrigation of each district is the concern and property of the community as a whole, administered by a committee with religious sanctions and ritual and special temples, called Subak. A certain amount of coffee and tobacco is also grown, as well as coconuts and a great variety of delicious fruits, chief among them being the pumilow—like a giant grape-fruit—and the mangosteen.

Of the aristocracy I only know by hearsay. They comprise about six per cent of the population and are divided into three castes—the Brahmins and Pedandas, or priests, the Satryas, or knights and princes, and the Vesia or rich merchants and land-owners. The rest of the population call themselves Wong Djaba, outsiders; the caste business is not for them. It is possible that the life of the aristocracy is as different from that of the rest of the population as Brahminism is from the Balinese religion. I doubt it, however, for they have left no apparent mark on the habits of the rest of the population; since the Hindu strain must be enormously diluted they probably are merely the richer Balinese. Their chief distinction is in their funerals. Such caste people as I met were actors or musicians.

The Balinese live in large patrilocal groups, a number of huts surrounded by a single magic wall to keep out evil spirits. Owing to the mildness of the Balinese climate—the sun is never dangerous, nor, save at midday, is the heat irksome—nearly the whole of life is lived in the open air, and houses are little more than sleeping-places, unpretentious and simple utilitarian buildings of wood and thatch; in the ordinary sense of the word there is no Balinese architecture, no roofed buildings. All their

ornamental and permanent constructions are walls
and gateways, built of red brick, with the stone work
of grey volcanic tuff, coated with " diamond " cement
to resist erosion.

The numberless temples are really sacred enclosures,
two or three courtyards surrounded by highly ornamented walls. The entrances to the different courtyards are all made after the same fashion ; the door
of the first court, Tchandi-bentar, is merely a gap ;
the walls rise on either side to an ornamental peak,
the inner surfaces being quite plain ; according to
legend the wall was originally whole but was cleft
by the gods who separated the two halves. The
entrance to the second courtyard, which must never
be on the same axis as the first, is a normal double-
panelled gateway, often very beautifully worked, and
set in an elaborate frame ; these entrances, Paduraksa, are only meant to be opened on special occasions, and there are small doorways at the side for
casual visitors, let in some way up the wall, so that
they have to be approached by steps. The last courtyard is the most sacred place.

In the temple courtyards are roofed meeting-places
for the elders, small square shrines for offerings, and
pagoda-like structures called Meru, mountains of the
gods, with an uneven number of black roofs, from
three to eleven, the top roof being the perch for the
god when he descends ; for the Balinese consider
that the higher gods—as opposed to those localised
in different springs and mountains—only visit their

Balinese Temple Gates:
Tchandi-bentar

shrines when called down on special occasions by the correct ritual.

The physical beauty of the Balinese has to my mind been greatly exaggerated by people who have written about them. They are well-made and healthy looking ; actual ugliness among them is uncommon, but so is outstanding beauty. I know of at least half a dozen races in different parts of the world where in an ordinary crowd you will find more satisfying physical types. The reputation of the Balinese is, I believe, founded on two facts ; firstly, they photograph extremely well, their brown and even skin, with the contrasting hair and well-marked features being pre-eminently photogenic ; and, secondly, both sexes habitually go naked except for a sarong. A typical Frenchman wrote in the Bali Hotel's visitors' book : " L'hôtel du soin ; l'Ile du sein," and from many visitors' point of view he has said everything. Female breasts are considered to be sexually stimulating ; those of the Balinese, though often rather broad, are firm and round and well-shaped ; if Josephine Baker could be induced to settle in the country you would have a non-stop revue à grand spectacle, with a personnel even larger than that of the Folies-Bergère under Lemarchand.

The Balinese are a very hermaphroditic race ; both sexes wear the same bright sarongs ; in the outlying villages both sexes wear their hair long, and ornament it with the scarlet hibiscus ; there is little difference in height between them ; both have fairly broad

shoulders and relatively narrow hips, so that from a
back view it is very difficult to distinguish ; the
breast muscles of many of the men are so developed
that even when they are seen from the front con-
fusion is justifiable. Many of the older men have
faces of great intellectual dignity.

Their faces are very expressive, frank and open,
quick to smile ; they are happy and unfrightened,
unsuspicious. This radiance is more stimulating
than any beauty.

With the advantages of soil and climate the work
of cultivation is not arduous ; after the business of
getting a living is done with the Balinese have
sufficient leisure to cultivate whatever arts they
favour, either as practitioners or audience. Lest any
of my readers should thereby condemn them as
arties I hasten to add that they kill animals for
pleasure, and are therefore worthy of all respect as
sportsmen. The strongest and commonest passion
of the Balinese is cock-fighting ; although it is now
forbidden by the Dutch Government on account of
the accompanying gambling, save on the rarest
occasions, this prohibition fares little better than the
Eighteenth Amendment did ; there are numberless
speak-easies for the sport hidden from the eye of
authority. And the commonest sight on the roads
in Bali in the afternoon is a man holding his rooster
in his arms and caressing it, or carrying it along in
the open-work bamboo cloche-shaped basket in which
the birds are habitually kept.

Cock-fights resemble greyhound races in that you want to take care not to sneeze at the crucial moment or you miss everything ; indeed neither of them usually last as long as a really good sneeze. The cocks have sharp steel spurs—about a quarter of an inch thick and four inches long—fastened to their legs ; although they sometimes take some time before they decide to attack one another the battle is usually extremely short ; a scurry of feathers and one of the birds is dead. If they absolutely refuse to clinch the combatants are shut up together for a short time under one of the baskets. For the onlooker the chief charm of these performances lies in the dramatic vivacity of the audience. The Balinese are also said to organise cricket-fights, but I never witnessed this.

The outstanding characteristic of the Balinese however is their love of art in every form. For them art is merely one of the manifestations of religion, and to separate the two is to create a false dichotomy ; their religion, however, is so complicated that for the sake of simplicity I prefer to treat the arts as though they were separate manifestations ; I hope later that they will fall into their proper place in Balinese life. The Balinese may be described as a nation of artists, professional if you take their attitude to their work into account, amateur if you consider their secondary (most especially financial) objectives. They are also a nation of keen critics ; our chauffeur, when we were looking at and buying wood carvings

and drawings, estimated the æsthetic value of the
different pieces offered to us with far sounder and
more reasoned judgment than that shown by most
European critics. The crowds which listen to the
complicated orchestral music and watch the highly
stylised dancing show that they are appreciative of
the slightest technical inventions or faults. Balinese
art is extremely local ; each village has its own
orchestra, its own dancers, its particular style of
carving or painting. Above all Balinese art is living,
in a constant state of development ; in all forms
the classical tradition is maintained, but the classics
are not worshipped as untouchable perfections ; they
are the foundations on which modern improvements
and alterations can be built, an attitude which I can
only parallel in English dramatists in the sixteenth
and seventeenth centuries. The Balinese have a
sense of and reverence for the past ; but it is part of
them and not, as with us, alien ; they have not
feelings either of humility or superiority towards the
work of their forefathers, though if you pressed them
I think they would admit that they were improving
on all that had gone before—the only healthy feeling
in art, except in coteries dead in Europe for the last
fifty years.

I think Dr. Stutterheim chose the right adjective
when he described Balinese stone sculpture as baroque.
It has the exuberance, the effervescence, and the
richness which we associate with the later southern
baroque art. The most elaborate stone carvings are

the doorways to the temples, most especially the royal Paduraksa. The architraves of these are often most elaborate, rising in a steep triangle, often divided into "wings" like a conventionalised pine-tree. Some motives are always associated with these gates, notably the large demon-face, or Bhoma, immediately above the centre of the gate and the dancing Shiva above that; but the rest of the façade is decorated according to the taste of the sculptors and the community; sometimes other large figures will be carved, sometimes legends on a smaller scale; others again will merely be decorated with flower and leaf motifs, or with intricate conventional designs. The grey stone is always combined with red bricks, a very pleasant effect; Balinese architecture is really garden architecture, and as such could be used extremely effectively.

A little behind the gates is erected a stone screen, to keep away evil spirits; spirits can only travel in a straight line, and such a screen prevents them advancing further, should they get in the gate; these screens are elaborately carved in low relief, usually with monsters to terrify any approaching demon.

Besides the gates the surrounding walls are often decorated with low-relief panels and with solid figures placed on the pediments. Shrines for offerings are also elaborately worked, and adorned with reliefs and supporting figures. The most usual style of such figure carvings is somewhat florid and curved, very

E

lively and though often somewhat grotesque never alarming ; there are however some very curious departures from the norm, some reliefs appearing to be almost purely Chinese, while one or two seem completely Mexican, both in conception and execution. If they were only a little more frequent and antique they would be splendid arguments for the " lost continent " theorists. The sculptures are occasionally crudely coloured. On the whole the best carvings, both in stone and wood, can be found in the south and centre of the island ; the north and west incline too strongly to " ginger bread " over-elaboration.

All the wood carving I saw was extremely modern ; in fact some of the pieces which we brought back were still unfinished the first time we saw them. Balinese wood-carving, like Balinese painting, has fairly recently undergone a profound modification ; the artists are relying more on direct observation and less on interior vision. They are still dominated to a very great extent by their mythology ; but in painting they are making their mythological figures more human and placing them against the background of their own village and countryside, instead of portraying them inhuman and in a void—the difference between Italian painters and their Byzantine predecessors—; and in sculpture, besides images of the gods, they are portraying their neighbours, and the birds and beasts around them. This change may possibly have been actuated by the influence and demands of Europeans,

Balinese Temple Gates:
Padu Raksa

and undoubtedly a certain amount of small carvings are turned out for the tourist trade ; it has however greatly enriched the vision of the Balinese artist. Most of the carvers and painters are peasants, and work as craftsmen ; if, however, you see the work of one man, still more if you talk with him, you will find that both by his personal vision and by his attitude to his work he is no different in essential quality to his European colleagues. He is a creative artist—not, as among the African negroes, a magician.

The Balinese carver shows an extraordinary sensitivity to his medium ; he employs the quality and grain of the wood with the greatest skill. The carvers who pleased me best go in for the greatest possible simplification, though except in the treatment of the hair this does not entail stylisation ; although the surface of the bird reproduced is smooth, the movement in the carving and the grain of the wood indicate feathers more vividly than any surface work. One sculptor had a peculiarly personal vision, all his figures being elongated and dramatic, reminiscent of El Greco ; his figures were carvings of grief, mostly in old people ; he was uninterested in the beauty of his subjects. Unfortunately the piece we brought back does not photograph well. It is chiefly round Tabanan and Gianjar that these modern artists live ; at Kloengoeng and Singaradja they keep more to the old style, elaborating the technique in carving further and further, becoming more and more intricate and over-elaborated, in a style which I personally find unpleasant.

Balinese painting and drawing has undergone much the same kind of modification. All the older paintings are temple hangings on cloth, or manuscripts (though most manuscripts are written on lontar leaves) ; some of the modern ones are on canvas fixed to stretchers in the European way. The drawings are made on paper with Chinese ink ; the brush is used as well as the pen.

The earlier paintings were of figures in the void without a background ; they are brightly coloured with a great deal of gold paint for the deities, slightly grotesque though technically very competent ; many of them are to European eyes extremely obscene.

As far as my inadequate observation goes the attitude of the Balinese to sex is quite unparalleled elsewhere ; they have neither modesty nor immodesty; they are in no way romantic about sex ; they treat it as any other part of the ordinary business of life ; it has no more intrinsic emotional importance to them than eating. This seems to me the only rational approach ; we all have to eat to keep well, and we enjoy our food ; we find a person who over-eats or is always thinking and talking about his food or indulges in odd diets absurd and disgusting and rather funny ; greedy people lack a sense of proportion. For food substitute whatever word you use for sexual activity and I think you will have a very fair idea of the attitude of the Balinese. To continue the metaphor, they enjoy a mixed diet, though there are some exoticisms that they regard in the same way as most Englishmen regard the swallowing of snails or frogs.

As might be expected, such an attitude leads to fidelity in later married life ; marriage made after such free selection is generally founded on physical harmony ; choice is based on reason and selection ; usually there is little reason to change. I also think it performs a useful service for the Balinese by separating the ideas of love and sexual intercourse ; while pleasure in the latter is almost a universal phenomenon, love I believe to be much rarer ; I doubt whether the ecstasy of love is commoner than the ecstasy of music or the other arts. A few people have a genius for love, but were it not for the example of art and literature and social expectation, I do not think it would be considered, as it is now, a universal phenomenon. With the highest and most lasting ecstasies love and sexual intercourse coincide for the Balinese, as for everyone else ; they admit, however —an important concession—that they can exist separately.

Such an attitude to sex is very valuable socially ; when such acts are not given any special importance the causes for personal friction, jealousy, disapproval, and censoriousness are considerably lessened. Even if it were true, as many would argue, that such an attitude is cheapening and degrading, it has socially so many compensations as to be very desirable.

One painting which I saw, which was too big to bring away, gives an admirable example of this attitude. It was a very pleasant picture of Balinese boys in shorts and shirts playing football. Along the touch-line a number of spectators of both sexes in their ordinary dress were watching the game, all except one man who had turned his back on the game (and towards the front of the picture) and lifting his sarong was in the midst of indulging in sensual solipsism. Besides the obvious satirical comment intended (that watching other people perform is a kind of masturbation) the conditions in which an artist can introduce such a figure into a serious picture perfectly normally without even considering that it may have any effect on the audience—just as the pictured man's behaviour was completely ignored by the other figures on the canvas —show, I think, a degree of sanity to which no other race that I know of can pretend.

Except for this painting and a couple of landscapes all the oils I saw were of mythological subjects. The modern Balinese painter uses a very sombre palette, considerably lowering all the observed tones. This is, I think, probably the only way of coping with tropical sunlight and vegetation ; the two European painters—Gauguin and Rousseau the douanier—who have painted successfully tropical landscapes have used the same dull tones. And certainly the realistic oils and water-colours, which artistic Dutchmen and other Europeans produce with such prolixity, are complete failures both as compositions and communications.

The line is still very important for Balinese painters, and, despite their medium, their paintings could mostly be described as coloured drawings. The chief peculiarity of Balinese artists, from the European point of view, is their attitude to perspective ; they appear to have the necessary technical ability for what we consider normal perspective ; they generally employ however what I can only describe as several perspectives in the same picture—that is to say that different parts of the picture appear to have been composed from different viewpoints ; in the mythological picture reproduced, for example, the wall and flowers and fountains in the foreground are seen by somebody placed immediately in front of them, while the inside of the pool and the bathers have been seen from above and from the left ; the flowers and trees at the back have been seen partly from the front and partly from on top, while the monkeys at the top of the picture have been seen from below. Provided the whole is satisfactory I see no reason to dub this device of varying perspective illegitimate, though it is rather disconcerting. This picture and the Kris dancers (see Illustrations facing pages 96 and 104) are drawings in Chinese ink ; the extraordinary technical ability is, I hope, evident even after double reproduction.

Of Balinese literature and humour I can say nothing at all, for the most obvious of reasons ; for the same reason I can say very little about their drama. As a dramatist I refuse to believe that a spectator, however intelligent, can really grasp much of a play whose language he does not understand. If this claim, which is sometimes made, is founded on anything except snobbery there is obviously no need for a dramatist to write words at all. He should score his parts like a musician.

The Balinese drama is divided into five cycles, each with slightly varying traditions and technique. Each cycle is founded on one of the great Hindu epics—the Tchalon-arang on the history of King Erlangga, the Parwa and the Wayong Wong on the Mahabharata (in which is included the Ramayana), the Gambuh and Tantri on the story of Pandji. Each village which has a dramatic company will specialise on one episode from one of these cycles, refining and improving to as great an extent as possible. The obvious parallel to this wealth of dramas derived from three epics is the tragedies of the Athenians.

Besides the characters and central anecdotes the five types of drama differ from one another in the costumes worn, the amount of masks—if any—employed, the sex of the players, and the type of orchestra which supplies the accompanying music. For the Balinese acting is a branch of dancing ; although there was no singing in any of the plays I saw music was almost continuous, and some of the parts—notably the gods—were entirely mimed ; even with speech trained and controlled movements illustrated the emotions. The Balinese are as much natural actors as the Italians ; the rigorous training to which they are subjected has turned their bodies

A Balinese Temple sculpture
in stone
(*cf. Chinese carvings*)

into extremely expressive instruments. Their movements are stylised and not " natural " ; they are most cunningly used, however, to enhance the effect desired. A king walking slowly on the points of his toes has a strange dignity which no amount of lighting and drapery will give him. For a person who does not understand the dialogue the most striking part of Balinese drama is the extraordinary nobility with which royal and divine rôles are rendered.

Nearly every important and dignified character is accompanied by a comic double or servant ; he speaks in prose while the noble character speaks in verse, in common language instead of the literary idiom ; he succumbs, or tries to succumb, to all the temptations the noble man must spurn, to all the weaknesses a noble character does not acknowledge ; it is as though every Pamino were accompanied by a Papageno, every King Henry by a Falstaff. The parallel with the *Magic Flute* is the nearer, for, as in that opera, many of the scenes are acted twice—once seriously and once in burlesque. This is slightly less disconcerting than might be thought, for the comic characters stay in their rôles ; it has the great advantage of keeping the dramas alive and real to the audience, preventing the classics ossifying or being treated with unsuitable reverence. Some of the burlesque is extremely subtle ; a comic houri in the story of Ardjuna, for example, performed a classical dance with something slightly wrong with every movement :

the eyes and the neck or the fingers and the wrist were unco-ordinated, instead of moving in harmony, as they should do. Most of the errors were very slight, for me almost imperceptible ; for the audience they were hugely comic. I was told, and can well believe, that this parody was far harder to learn and perform than the proper dance.

Besides plays the Balinese have the shadow and puppet shows, as in Java. I also saw an extraordinarily good performance by one man, which reminded me of similar performances by Ruth Draper ; he acted a complete play, taking all the rôles in turn, changing his voice for each character, and putting on masks, or parts of masks, and wigs for each change. This Topeng, as it is called, was a remarkable exhibition of virtuosity.

Although all Balinese dancing is dramatic there are some dances in which the dramatic interest takes so much precedence over the choreographic that they can more properly be treated as pantomime. Such is the Barong—the dance of a mythical monster, consisting of a bamboo frame transformed with fibre and cloth and mirrors into a highly fantastic lion or tiger, under which two men dance, sometimes accompanied by masked demons and clowns (Djaook and Topeng). They are lively interludes, often to be seen on village roads and temples in the evening, but of little interest as dancing. The Djanger dance is also more of a pantomime. It is the newest Balinese dance, and is often referred to as the Balinese jazz ;

it was apparently invented in 1920, and was a great
favourite among the youths' and unmarried-girls'
clubs.   There are an equal number of boys and girls ;
the girls sit in two lines facing one another, and the
boys join up the square ; in the centre is the leader,
or Dag, an older man.   The Dag sings the story of
some mythological episode, and the others take the
part of chorus, moving their arms, heads, and bodies
in unison ; boys and girls, however, never make the
same movements at the same time.   There is a little
pantomime at the more dramatic moments, when
members of the chorus act rudimentary rôles, going
into the centre of the square to do so.   The charm of
this performance, such as it is, lies chiefly in the
costumes and make-up ; the girls have rather a
handsome " Spanish " make-up of pale ochre ; their
eyebrows are shaved and artifically marked, and their
hair dressed and greased so that it lies flat on
the forehead and rises behind into a thin bun
which is decorated with flowers ; the loose ends
fall down their back.   They wear thick baton-
like earrings, and a diadem made of bamboo and
metal studded with fresh frangipani blossoms.   Round
their necks they have metallic bibs, and they are
swathed in tight-fitting bright dresses.   The boys take
less trouble ; they wear a cloth bandeau in their
hair, and blue sarongs with a deep waist-band, rising
half-way up the breast.   Like so many non-European
races the Balinese put on more clothes when they
wish to celebrate or to appear particularly alluring.

They appear to enjoy this extremely sedate performance very much. (It seems probable that the famous
" kris " dance, though performed in trance, is also
chiefly of a dramatic nature ; but I had no opportunity to see a performance.)

I have two difficulties in writing about Balinese
music, one particular, and one general ; I only
heard one composition repeated, of the score or so
pieces of orchestral music I heard ; and I am anyhow
incompetent to write about music without the
presence of an orchestral score, a pianist, and a
musically-knowledgeable companion. I am sorry
about this, for Balinese music is very well worth
writing about. There are five types of orchestra, or
Gamelan, of increasing complexity and variety,
besides accompaniments of various combinations of
instruments to the different dramatic performances.
The orchestras consist entirely of percussion instruments, chiefly of metal with the exception of the
Gamelan Gambang, or bamboo orchestra. The
assorted gongs, cymbals, drums, and so on have an
enormous variety of pitch and timbre ; there is not
the contrast in texture that there is in a full European
orchestra, but there is more richness and variety
than in any partial combination, such as strings or
wind instruments. The Balinese tone-scale—I write
under correction—is the tonic, though on occasion
they use a four-note scale ; they employ half and
quarter tones to a considerable extent.

Balinese music, like the other Balinese arts, is a

Balinese sculpture in stone
*A Dutch sailor: on the law-court
at Kloengoeng*

living body ; the classics are admired and played, but modern compositions, founded on and improving the older music, enjoy as great if not greater favour. Formally it is of the greatest complexity, employing such devices as the double and triple fugue, and a rather complicated variation of the sonata form ; a Balinese orchestral piece is usually in four or five movements. From the formal point of view the comparison between Balinese music and the works of J. S. Bach is inescapable ; in orchestral colour it is nearer the later works of Debussy, who is said to have been strongly influenced by the far-eastern music he had heard at some colonial exhibition. Speaking as a musical amateur I should say that Balinese music is by far the most interesting and pleasant music being composed to-day.

The Balinese have worked out, I am told, a system of musical notation, but it is comparatively seldom used. When a composer works out a new piece— with much the same disturbance and irritability as a European artist—he establishes the composition in his head, using the large gong as a European composer does the piano, and then teaches each member of the orchestra in turn ; he conducts the new composition himself, facing the orchestra, which is seated in a double rank round three sides of a square, and marking the tempi with a drum. A full orchestral work takes about six months to compose and rehearse.

The musicians are naturally chiefly poor peasants. Every village has its own orchestra, often with local

variations in the balance and tuning of the instruments ;
the population as a whole has the same knowledge of
and feeling for musical subtlety as the Czechs appear
to have had in Mozart's time.   Mijnheer Potjewyd,
the manager of the Bali hotel, whose sudden death
has robbed Balinese music of one of its chief patrons
and enthusiasts, had instituted for his private pleasure
and at his own cost a Balinese musical festival, and
gave prizes for the best new compositions, the best
playing of a set piece, and the best technique, the
judgment being made by a jury of Balinese.

Much Balinese music is accompanied by a male
dancer, seated inside the hollow square formed by
the musicians.   This dancer wears a flowered head-
dress ; his body up to the breasts is swathed in a
length of embroidered cloth, and he wears a sarong
made of a wide and rich material, of which about
two yards lies on the ground to his left.   The manipu-
lation of this piece of stuff is an intrinsic part of the
dance.   In his right hand the dancer holds a fan ;
while the finger-nails of his left hand are allowed to
grow to a considerable length.   During the whole
dance the man never stands up ; to change position
he raises his body slightly and moves over the ground
with his legs still crossed.

Balinese dancing is nearly as exclusively occupied
with the upper half of the body as European dancing
is with the lower half.   The movements of the legs
are relatively unimportant and of little interest ; on
the whole the body from the breast to the feet is

treated as a unit, always keeping on the same plane and making a single line ; with a little exaggeration it may be said that Balinese dancing starts from the shoulders upward. The technique of Balinese dancing is excessively refined and meticulous, extraordinarily subtle ; it is built up on the harmonious relationships of the movements of the shoulder, the forearm, the elbow, the wrist, the hand and the fingers (either treated together or as separate units), the neck, the head, the eyes, and the facial expression. A number of the movements have to be acquired in earliest youth, and are impossible for people who have not been so trained ; such are the displacement of the head to one side while the neck is kept rigid, and the extraordinary counterpoint of wrist, hand, and fingers. The training of Balinese dancers begins before they can walk ; walking, in fact, forms the first part of the training. Incidentally the walk of the Balinese, especially the women, is extraordinarily graceful, and a continuous pleasure to watch.

With this very subtle technique the Gamelan dancer accompanies and illustrates the music, sometimes dispassionately, making visible the orchestral forms, sometimes dramatically, the emotions of the music passing like reflections over the mobile face, sometimes in stylised pantomime. This type of dancing requires greater training than any other and is usually performed by grown men ; on one occasion however I saw a small boy of nine perform ; he was extremely self-possessed and efficient, but he made a

number of faults in technique—his eyes and fingers
particularly were not sufficiently co-ordinated—which
made his performance slightly comic to the onlookers.
This embodiment of the music adds enormously to
the general effect, as though Toscanini had the
technique of Lifar.

Probably the most popular, and certainly the best
known of all Balinese dances is the Legong, a legend
acted by two or three children in stylised pantomime.
The children are dressed in cloth of gold, with large
metallic head-dresses studded with fresh flowers.
The children portray a series of characters elegantly
and gracefully ; it is a very pretty spectacle. On the
whole Balinese girls do not dance after they have
reached puberty ; and Balinese dancing is unique,
as far as my knowledge goes, in having no apparent
erotic appeal at all.

The two most impressive performances I saw in Bali
were religious ceremonies, performed in temples. The
first is called Sang-yang. One of the communities
of Denpasar had had continuous ill-fortune, and so to
soften the hearts of the gods dances were held during
the nights of the full moon. Two little girls, aged
about six, knelt in front of braziers on which various
herbs were being burnt. To the accompaniment of
a woman's chanting they swayed their heads rhythmically over the braziers, their long hair sweeping
the ground. This movement was performed from the
waist and continued for a long time, perhaps the
better part of an hour, till the children fell back rigid

in a trance. They were then washed in holy water, their hair was dressed, and they were clothed in gorgeous sacerdotal clothes, and sacred head-dresses, heavy with jewels and flowers, were placed on their heads and fans put in their hands. The children suffered this unmoving, with eyes shut. Then, when they were ready they were lifted on to mats in the centre of the courtyard, and the congregation, seated around, started singing holy songs. The little girls danced in absolute unison, moving together like marionettes held by the same wire, following every change of rhythm and emotion and speed in the singing, as though the music were the wire that moved them. All the time the moon was up they danced without rest, their eyes closed ; sometimes a girl would drop her fan, unconsciously, for her empty hand continued the gestures ; the fan would be purified over the braziers, and then the tiny fingers closed over it again. For the greater part of the night they danced, sometimes savagely, sometimes majestically, following the songs, perfect in technique ; as the moon went down they took gourds of holy water and sprinkled the assembly with it.

The physical feat of dancing for so many hours without pause seemed to me extraordinary, and I aske if the children weren't exhausted by such an effort ; I was told that they felt absolutely no fatigue. The girls are chosen while still infants, for a child who will be a Sang-yang dancer will fall into a trance in her mother's arms when she hears the music or smells

F

the incense. This trance-dancing has extraordinary majesty, as though the body of the child were indeed filled with the divine spirit.

The Katchak is also used to avert calamity, the men of the village uniting to produce the necessary oracular trance in one of their number. Since Bedoelen, where we saw this performed, was at the moment prosperous, the ceremony stopped short of its real objective, a small stylised dance replacing the trance revelations.

At night in the temple courtyard a tall lantern with three wicks is placed in the centre. Around this all the adult males of the community sit in concentric circles, perhaps two hundred in all, naked except for a short sarong, with red hibiscus in their hair, which, if it is long, falls loosely down their back. In unison they start to sing, and accompany their singing with rhythmic movements. The song is wild and varied in rhythm, and their voices rich and true so that the sound has the volume of an organ ; as the ritual reaches its climax the musical quality is discarded for strange rhythmic noises, the sound of machines and thunder, the magical *Hik* of the Thibetan lamas. For the greater part of the ritual the crowd moves absolutely as one man, now one arm describing a curve, now all the hands high in the air and the thousand fingers moving rhythmically like the sea churned by breezes, now all falling back with the arms at the sides palm upwards, overlaying one another to form a huge rose, each petal a naked human torso. As the

Balinese Temple bas-relief
(*cf. Mexican bas-reliefs*)

ritual reaches its climax the crowd divides into two halves, each side rising in turn, those nearest the middle crouching, and each rank rising higher till the outermost are on tip-toe, accompanying their guttural noises with violent and dramatic gestures. This interplay between the two halves continues faster and faster, the human force now in another dimension, agitated more and more violently ; until one is possessed and rushes to the centre between the two contending groups ; as he speaks the circles are re-formed, and when he is done the singing ends as it started.

Although for the European spectator the Sang-yang dancers and the Katchak are artistic spectacles of the most moving and exciting quality, they are not so regarded by the Balinese ; they are religious rituals, with no place in them for the non-participating spectator. Art addresses an audience, whose sole function is appreciation and criticism ; in ritual the audience also has its part.

In all religions four functions can be recognised : an ethical system, a mythology, a ritual, and religious experience. In primitive and homogeneous communities these four functions may be inextricably combined into a single whole ; in societies of greater complication and development they often become widely separated and mutually contradictory, so that one or more functions becomes over-developed while the others atrophy either partially or completely ; thus with Judaism and Protestantism the greatest emphasis is laid on the ethical system ; with Roman Catholicism on mythology and ritual ; and with many forms of Buddhism and Hinduism on religious experience.

The religion of Bali is made extraordinarily complicated by the fact that their mythology has no connection whatsoever with their ritual and religious experience. Their mythology, with very slight modifications, they have taken from the Hindus ; in their arts it is the story of the Hindu gods and heroes which is always at the base of their themes ; but in the temples, although Vishnu, Shiva, Brahma, and the other inhabitants of the Hindu pantheon may receive a small shrine (and that by no means always), yet they have very little part in the worship ; the Brahmin priest, or Pedanda, is only allowed to be present at certain festivals ; the Balinese—at any rate the people : I know nothing about the aristocracy—have made use of the Hindu mythology for their own artistic ends ; with slight modifications their religion is still in the pre-Hindu state, mystical, " animistic," magical.

I am too ignorant to be able to discuss the Balinese ethical system, and the influence of Hinduism on it, in any detail. As far as I can see they have not a strong theocratic ethical system, but that may be my personal prejudice, seeing what I want to see ; for to my mind theocratic sanctions in a mobile (as opposed to a static) community are socially extremely undesirable ; their origin makes them intolerably rigid, with the result that either great distress and friction is forced on the people living under such laws (for example present-day India or seventeenth-century Spain and England), or else there is a complete divorce between theory and practice (as in the whole of the Christian world to-day) with the result that people, no longer impressed by the out-moded and illogical sanctions of the Church, place no restraint whatsoever on their greed and lusts, beyond what the man-made laws impose on them, thereby hurling themselves, and with them the community, into the abyss of anarchical horror.

The chief impact of Hinduism on Balinese practice that I can see is the taboo on cow's flesh; this is not however extended to the other ruminants, such as the caribou. The burial rites are also much influenced by Hinduism.

Balinese life and religion is founded on the village as a community; their ethics are dictated by the benefit or harm which would accrue to the community as a whole were certain acts performed; judgments and punishments when necessary (except now when such matters directly regard the colonisers) are given by the elders of the village sitting in council in the village temple. Such anti-social acts as theft or murder or impiety are severely punished; if people did not do their share of the work for the community they would probably be deprived of the benefits therefrom; but, as far as I can see, the Balinese do not interfere with private behaviour which does not influence other members of the community. Women, especially married women, are in a fairly subordinate position.

Before discussing Balinese ritual it is necessary to say something about the religious experience from which it is derived. This question of religious experience has been for me all my life a subject of the greatest fascination ; I have read all that has come my way on the subject and have written two (unacted) plays about it. My experiences in West Africa a year ago gave me some concrete material to work on ; and I have now in my own mind a theory which seems to me to be a basis for further investigation, and, as a theory, to take into account a number of manifestations which have always escaped any mechanistic or materialistic system of psychology or philosophy. With some trepidation I am going to make a rough sketch of this theory ; I do not intend what I write to mean more than it says ; I am only advancing a hypothesis, not founding a movement ; this hypothesis entails an unfashionable dualistic view of human nature ; it is almost entirely unsupported by scientific, as opposed to anecdotal, evidence ; and it is to a great extent unsatisfactory as it seems at the moment extremely difficult to disprove.

Although I disagree with nearly all of William James's conclusions, he performed a very useful service in collating the writings of the mystics of the three chief religions in the *Varieties of Religious Experience :* any reader of that book, much more any reader

Modern Balinese carvings in wood
of mythological subjects

of the original documents, cannot but help being struck by the fact that although the creeds and mythologies believed in by the different mystics he quotes are very different and often contradictory, yet the experiences and the way they are obtained are so similar that until you come to the end you do not know if you are reading a Christian or a Buddhist or a Sufi mystic. Owing to his belief in moral progress, and probably also through the influence of that delightful, but often very misleading writer, Sir James Frazer, James dismissed the manifestations of less organised religions—whether primitive or heretical— as barbarisms ; thereby, to my mind, depriving himself of the one possible clue which could unravel the tangle into which he had got himself.

I wish to suggest, as a hypothesis, that man is a machine with two functions. The best analogy which presents itself to me is that of a radio-gramophone ; the radio-gramophone, employing largely the same materials in both cases, can either make music with things (wax discs), or pick music out of the air. As an analogy this is not particularly satisfactory, for it gives the impression of a categorical alternative, which in the case of man does not exist ; it would be more satisfactory if we knew nothing of wave mechanics, or the connection between the radio and the music played elsewhere ; it is however the best I can find, and has a certain use.

In Europe to-day we are normally all gramophones —that is to say we are, at any rate ideally, scientific and rational, dealing exclusively with measurable things ; we treat the phenomenal universe as the only real one. This purely objective life breaks down in patches ; some people still have religious experience, a few still produce and enjoy art, " psychic phenomena " occasionally break in.

In West Africa, on the other hand, and in Thibet, as described by Madame David-Neel, people are nearly all radios ; they act in a way which goes against logic and reason ; and they treat the phenomenal universe as supremely unimportant, and in a way subjective ; as I have said before, if we are sane they are mad.

It is very hard to describe concisely what I mean by " being a radio," for it is an unscientific and irrational conception ; to put it as simply as I can I consider that the human mind is always potentially a source of energy, and that by special training this energy can be enormously increased in power. I propose calling this energy M.E., to stand for Mental, or Mystical or Magical Energy, as you will. To the extent that it can be observed and measured this energy does not obey any of the laws of physics that we know ; beyond the fact that those who have developed it believe that it moves in a straight line, it does not seem to be influenced by space, nor, within certain limits, by time.

It seems as though M.E. were about as evenly distributed as a musical sense. A very few people are tone-deaf ; the majority can recognise a tune and sing more or less in key, and can *by training* become competent musicians ; a few, more talented, can " pick out a tune " on whatever instrument they are used to, without any teaching ; and occasionally geniuses are born with an apparently innate knowledge of music. Using this parallel, I should say that the great religious teachers of the world were geniuses; the activities recorded by Mr. Charles Fort in *Wild Talents*, the stories of Mozarts born in music-less communities; the doings in so far as they are genuine investigated by the Society for Psychical Research, and similar bodies, the work of people who can " pick out a tune " ; and most mystics and magicians whose experiences have been recorded the trained executants. Very recently a Dr. Rhine in Carolina has been investigating the people who can sing more or less in key but who have had no proper training ; his book, *Extrasensory Perception*, gives the record of an enormous number of experiments on telepathy and clairvoyance carried on with a number of students intermittently under laboratory conditions ; he worked with five cards in groups, and found that by concentration these students could name these cards when they were looked at by somebody else, whether in their presence or not, or when shuffled and placed in front of them, with a far greater percentage of correct guesses than could be obtained by pure chance. Actually, over a series of ninety thousand experiments, the students named correctly a little over two in every five, instead of the one which pure

chance would indicate. These experiments have
been very useful in establishing the facts statistically ;
they tell us very little about the principles involved.
It seems to me certain that Dr. Rhine will not get a
higher correlation with correctness while working
with ordinary students.

The mystics of the various schools and churches
have left complete instructions as to how to develop
M.E. Two preliminary conditions are essential : the
neophyte must believe such development possible and
desirable ; and the phenomenal universe must have
no emotional importance to him. It is this second
condition which makes the development and consequent investigation of M.E. in our civilisation so
difficult ; for we are both by education and practice
attached emotionally to people and things all our
lives ; we consider those who are not inhuman. It
is, however, an indispensable condition, repeatedly
emphasised by Jesus, by the Buddha, by the West
African fetisher : you cannot serve God and Mammon ;
you must take no thought for the morrow. The
importance of the phenomenal world is usually
destroyed by asceticism, but it can on occasion be
accomplished by the greatest cold-blooded de-
bauchery, as some of the Christian heretics—the anti-
nomians and the pre-adamites, for example—some
Tantric sects, and probably the Bacchantes in Greece
showed.

Once these conditions are fulfilled the neophyte
develops M.E. by concentration. For this purpose

Modern Balinese carving in wood

he lives on a very light diet and stays in the same place, preferably in a desert or in a very subdued light for some time. During this period he concentrates his mind on one thing, apparently no matter what; the Buddhists give diagrams or formulas to concentrate on, latter-day magicians geometrical figures, the Jesuits and other Christian mystics visions of the Passion or the future life. The important part of this training lies apparently in fixing the will and attention on one interior vision for a very long time—incidentally an extraordinarily hard thing to do; this focussing apparently changes the quality of the mind, as concentrated light changes to heat. The non-Christian mystics add to this concentration various physical exercises, especially voluntary control of breathing; for the Christians the body is to be despised; for the others to be turned into a weapon. If their claims are justified certain Indians and Thibetans have apparently succeeded in controlling completely the ordinarily involuntary bodily processes. They can apparently also raise the bodily temperature at will so as to be impervious to cold (Thibetan *tumo*), sufficiently control the bloodstream to prevent bleeding from wounds (Mohammedan dervishes and Balinese kris dancers), and accomplish enormous physical labour without fatigue (Thibetan *lung-gom*). After a certain amount of training people practically dispense with sleep, and certainly never fall into a sleep which interrupts their special kind of consciousness.

The subjective effects of such training in concentration appear in a number of well-defined stages—for one of the most curious things about training for M.E. is that with it, as with intoxicating drugs, there is very little individual variation in the results obtained. The first stage is reached when objects seen subjectively have as much reality as objects seen ordinarily. This stage is both frightening and dangerous, often leading to madness ; for the neophytes are taught to believe in their visions as real, and to treat them as such. When this stage is prolonged the visions are conceived to be of the same quality as the objective world, both being illusions existing only in the mind of the perceiver—a form of solipsism apparently inevitable to all mystics. Further concentration destroys this feeling too, and the perceiver is no longer separated from the things perceived, the self from the not-self ; this loss of the feeling of individuality apparently brings with it a feeling of ineffable bliss, so strong that it alters and influences the lives of those who experience it for ever after. It is this feeling which is described in such halting language by the Christian mystics—St. Teresa, Pascal, St. Ignatius, and countless others. Generally after reaching this stage the neophytes return to ordinary life ; some, however, continue as hermits and push their concentration further still, breaking down stage after stage till they reach a completely indescribable but apparently overwhelmingly satisfying sense of Nothingness—*ein lautes Nichts*. It may be remarked that it is not necessary either to believe in God or the immortality of the soul to achieve these results ; Buddhism and Brahminism are both atheistic religions, and Buddhists of the " Short Path," who particularly practise such exercises, use them specifically to escape immortality and reincarnation.

These subjective experiences can be described as self-sought delusions ; they differ, however, from the delusions of drugs and fever by retaining all their strength for normal life. They also apparently create a communicable force in those who have induced them which is manifested in different ways—in the influence they have on others, in powers of healing, and in other ways which I will try to describe later. It may be noted that the leaders of the three great religions, Jesus, Mohammed, and Gautama, all went through a period of solitary contemplation and concentration *before* starting on their mission. I think also that it is possible to read the Gospels as the accounts of a man who, after such an experience, developed extraordinary M.E., and gave instructions to his followers how to do likewise. Under such an interpretation a great deal of the contradictions of the Gospels straighten out, for example, Jesus's insistence on the unimportance of the phenomenal world (Take all you have and give it to the poor— The poor you have always with you—Who are my father and mother?—My father and I are one), and on all observances of ethics and religion. More

important still is the emphatic The kingdom of
heaven is *within* you, together with all the negative
descriptions of heaven. The miracle-working powers
of Jesus also fall into place, including the little-
commented-on piece of clairvoyance with Nathaniel
(John I. 48).

For besides the subjective experiences caused by
the creation of M.E., this energy can be made to work
objectively in different and peculiar ways. It is here
that the greatest difficulties occur, for it is usually
only those who have imperfectly rid themselves of
the idea of the importance of the phenomenal world,
who have either the idea or the wish to exhibit these
powers, except in the most primitive communities
who have no scientific apparatus for dealing with
their environment, and therefore employ M.E. to an
extent unparalleled elsewhere.

The most generally granted functions of M.E. are
clairvoyance and telepathy, the ability to read
thoughts or see objects at a distance either in space
or time. With this goes a more questionable ability
to see the past and the future. Adepts are also
apparently able to influence objects at a distance
without any palpable means ; besides poltergeists
and so on there are the experiments of the S.P.R. on
Rudi Schneider and other untrained mediums. They
are also able to communicate their force to others by
direct contact, to strengthen and heal them ; on this
ability rest not only the actions of faith-healers, but
also the whole theory of priesthood and kingship ;

the priest or king is a source of energy for the community, and by ministrations and direct contact can impart this energy to their subjects or congregation ; without this theory such rites as the laying on of hands become meaningless, with it the idea of blessing understandable.   This energy can also apparently be transmitted through certain media, especially water, and I do not know of any religion in which holy water does not play a rôle ; it can also be imparted to other objects, but with far greater difficulty.

The strangest claim of all made for people with strong M.E. is the power to render the (consciously) illusory creations of their musings visible, and in some cases palpable to the rest of the world.   This power is specifically claimed by Indians and Thibetans, and Madame David-Neel describes the method of doing this among the lamas and also her own success in it.   She also says that the lamas (or some of them) account for ghosts and demons as being voluntarily created illusions which have sufficient vitality to continue apart from their creators.[1]   In this region, where common sense and logic and the laws of physics are banished, we have no guide beyond experience and the faith we place in the statements of others ;   I find this idea of created phantoms in many ways repulsive, and yet a satisfactory

[1] This activity is (if it exists) probably often unconscious : in West Africa wonder workers are controlled by relatively normal people.

explanation of ghosts and hauntings and many seeming miracles (including perhaps the panthers I saw in Dahomey).

I would like to suggest also that artistic creation is another function of M.E. The preliminary conditions—concentration and (to a certain extent) freedom from emotional contact with the phenomenal world—are the same ; the curious ecstasy of artistic creation, which will often drive artists against all their rational needs and desires, seems to be of the same nature as, though weaker than, the mystical ecstasy ; and no system of reason, of common sense, or of physics, has been able to account for the pleasure felt in artistic creations which may be completely alien or even repulsive to the common sense mind. (To take a personal example, the works of Milton and Dante, told in other words, seem to me repulsively stupid and irrational, the objects painted by Rembrandt often disgusting ; yet the pleasure I get from the works of these three people is of quite a different quality to that I get by reading people whose ideas seem to me sound and desirable, or by seeing the most pleasant objects.)

Such, then, is my hypothesis of M.E., put very briefly and simply. It is quite a useful hypothesis, for it gathers together a large number of disparate phenomena, including a meeting-ground for magic and religion. I refuse to believe that the greater part of the world, not only to-day but through all recorded history, has been engaged in rituals and practices

A modern Balinese drawing in Chinese
ink of a mythological subject

which have given absolutely no result; when I find a number of claims made entirely separately by people scattered all over history and geography I am willing to give them at any rate provisional belief.

From the accounts of the ceremonies already given it will be seen that the real Balinese religion is the cultivation and use of M.E. The Katchak was an attempt to acquire M.E. by collective action. The really important figure in Balinese ceremonies is the Pemangku, or village priest, in whom the M.E. of the community is concentrated. He was earlier, and is still occasionally, also the secular chief of the village. When the Hindu kings arrived they claimed also to possess M.E., and therefore demanded respect and post-mortem worship ; so they stripped the Pemangku of his secular authority and put another official in his place.

The Balinese ordinarily live very simply and frugally, and all their festivals are feasts—an admirable arrangement. Offerings are made to the gods, the local genii and spirits in the mountains and water and sun, of meat, fruit, and flowers ; these are placed before the shrine, so that the gods can extract their " essence", and then eaten by the offerers in a communal feast. The decorative ability displayed by the Balinese in arranging these offerings is very impressive ; fruit and flowers are arranged into the most elaborate still-lifes and abstract patterns. They also make most ingenious streamers from the leaves of the

G

banana, the palm, and the bamboo, plaiting and arranging them into very pleasant patterns and pictures.

Besides the temple festivals which are held for a variety of different occasions, there are also household festivals for birth, teeth-filing (when practised), marriage and death. The only festival of which I have any personal knowledge is the cremation ceremony, and there I only saw the burning of a caste-less man. When a man dies he is provisionally buried, or on occasion placed under the eaves of the house, while the survivors collect the necessary money for the very expensive cremation. When the cash is collected the body is exhumed and wrapped in a number of white cloths and laid on a bier in the house, while the Brahmin, clothed in a sugar-loaf hat and special vestments, chants mantra on a perch in the courtyard. A ceremonial chariot is constructed, chiefly of bamboo, and brightly ornamented with coloured paper, cloth, mirrors, artificial and real flowers, and numberless other fal-lals. In the case of the higher nobility these chariots have super-imposed roofs like a Meru, up to eleven in number, and make very imposing if fragile pagodas, sometimes from twenty to thirty feet in height. There is also constructed separately a casket, in the shape of an ithyphallic bull made of wood and covered with bright cloth or paper and wool-work. The horns, which are often detachable, are made of gilded wood, and the beast is also ornamented with gold lace. When the ceremony is ready to start the

Brahmin shoots four arrows to the four corners of the universe, and then a procession of the women carrying offerings sets off to the cremation field, while the men carry the chariot on which the corpse has been placed. The procession circles the field clockwise three times, and then the chariot is placed in the centre. The animal-shaped coffin is then brought in and the corpse transferred to it. But not easily, for the men divide themselves into two parties, representing good and wicked spirits, and a scrimmage takes place between them for the possession of the corpse. Since the corpse is often months old and fairly fragile it is not unknown for it to be broken to pieces in the tussle. After this undignified but apparently enjoyable scrum the corpse is placed in the bull, which is opened along the back to receive it, and the bull placed on the chariot ; the more valuable of the trappings are removed, and the whole structure fired with wood piled underneath it. When only ashes remain these are gathered up into an urn which is cast into the sea, or, if the cremation takes place inland, into a sea-going river, so that the body is twice purified, by fire and by water. During the ceremony music is performed on a special orchestra, and, sometimes, special dances performed. This is the only private ceremony at which the presence of a Brahmin priest, or Pedanda, is essential ; he is also always present at purification feasts, when a community is cleansed from the contagion of misfortune and " accident," and at the dedication of new temples. Otherwise his rôle is completely subordinate, his chief function being to " give tone " and to consecrate the holy water.

Nobody can be more conscious than I am of how inadequate the foregoing description of Balinese life is. My one hope is that it errs only by omission. I do not believe that one can give a really adequate account of the life of a people unless one can be completely concrete ; I think that it is far less valuable to say " This is how the people of X. act and believe," than to describe how A and B, inhabitants of X., act and think and talk in their daily lives. Generalisations applied to ourselves and our own people always strike us as foolish and inaccurate ; why should they be valid when applied to strangers ? There are so many facets and discrepancies in the life of a community that almost inevitably people concentrate on and exaggerate those which are congenial to them and to their ideas. It is questionable whether there is such a thing as the absolute truth about the life of a community ; but we can get nearer it if we can learn the lives of individual members of it.

There is, however, I think one generalisation that can be made about Bali ; the Balinese are a very happy people. Now for me the happiness of the group is the most important of all considerations ; so important that whenever I find it elsewhere I wish to see how it is achieved and whether any of the constituents are applicable for my own community. I can find little other than passing interest in activities which I cannot connect up with my own times and the interests of my community.

The Balinese start with great advantages in a congenial climate and a fertile soil ; nature has provided for them what machino-facture may one day provide for us : leisure. Their way of living and their sense of belonging to a community frees by far the greater number from anxiety and fear of starvation, or illness, or the condition of their dependents ; socialism may do as much for us. Among the population as a whole—for I cannot speak of the aristocracy —there is no feeling of superiority or inferiority, of inherent difference ; they are a democracy in as much as each man *feels* himself to be the equal of his neighbour, differing only in individual talents and abilities. Their conduct seems to be regulated by the two rules of King Pausole—the only ethical system for which I have any sympathy—though the interpretation of what harms our neighbour is both difficult and liable to great local variation. The void, which leisure and lack of anxiety, did they arrive to-morrow, would create in our lives, is filled with religion and art which derives from it.

The Balinese are extraordinarily fortunate in having

a mythology which is accepted for artistic purposes, but is not of emotional importance. The only other race that I know of who were in a similar position were the Athenians of the sixth and fifth centuries before Christ. The Homeric mythology supplied them with artistic motives ; magic, or M.E., supplied their real religion. We are so used to considering the Athenians as the best type of all-round Oxford don (with, perhaps, some rather regrettable habits) that we forget the important part that magic played in their lives, at any rate up to the time of Socrates. The Delphic oracle—in which incidentally Socrates appears to have believed—is the classic example of the use of an entranced person with highly developed M.E. for the benefit of the community. At Dodona and elsewhere there were secondary centres of M.E. The orgiastic sects were chiefly, and the Eleusinian mysteries entirely magical. It is difficult to appreciate the importance of the Mysteries, though the constant recurrence of their formulæ, particularly in the work of Æschylus and Plato, shows the supreme importance they held in at any rate some people's lives. (In the late eighteenth century freemasonry appears to have been equally important.) I would be prepared some other time to argue that the Mysteries were the chief source of the Athenian miracle, and also of its sudden extinction ; that, on account of their being secret rites, to exclude slaves, they formed, and then destroyed, the community.

I think a mythology is, if not essential, at any rate

of the very greatest help to an artistic tradition,
particularly a mythology which is treated with serious-
ness but not with reverence. The Christian mythologies—indeed all mythologies which have sprung
from Asia Minor—have been too lacking in shading,
too black-and-white, to be useful for literature or
drama, with very rare exceptions ; also they have
demanded too much belief. They have been among
the greatest inspirations for the plastic arts. In
English literature we can trace a series of secular
mythologies, or accepted beliefs ; first in a rational
idea of fate and the peculiar qualities of kings (Shake-
speare and his contemporaries), then in the supremacy
of reason (Pope and Dryden), the supremacy of
nature (the romantic revival), and to-day[1] in the
ecstasies of sexual love and violence, or (to use a
single word for both manifestations) in *thrills*. The
various uses of this word in current speech are
sufficiently indicative. People talk of the thrill
of love, the æsthetic thrill, the religious thrill,
the thrill of danger, the thrill of murder, and
robbery, and sudden death. Unfortunately we
believe in our mythologies instead of using them,
a disastrous and most dangerous situation. The
insistence to-day on the supreme ecstasy of sexual

[1] For a brilliant but extremely alarming description of modern
consciously created mythology and ritual in such groups as the
Y.M.C.A., Toc H., etc., see Harold Stovin's *Totem*. Although
he stresses particularly the myths of Fellowship and Fitness, the
sensationalism at the back of these movements is made sufficiently obvious (e.g., p. 165).

love is particularly nauseating and inescapable ; it is endlessly flaunted at us, in our books, in our plays, in our films, in our popular music. To emphasise this point I made a list of the songs sung for two evenings over the wireless and wrote down the most significant portions of the lyrics ; but to copy it out is too unpleasant ; anybody who doubts my contention can perform the same labour for himself. Now most people I think would agree that this non-stop harping on sex as the supreme joy is extremely unhealthy, especially as the law does everything possible to prevent people enjoying the heaven which is in their art so endlessly preached at them, so that most people are in a chronic state of unsatisfied sexual desire. The prophets of this attitude are Freud and D. H. Lawrence and their followers. What is particularly dangerous is that despite all the prohibitions of convention and law people do acquire sexual experience, and, for the greater part, find out that they have been stuffed with lies, that though pleasant, it is no such lasting ecstasy and final solution as art would leave us to suppose ; and then they are ready for the other half of our myth, violence.

There has never been a community so occupied with crime and murder and violence as the Western world to-day. After sex, crime is our great interest ; it is the motive for half our films and plays and literature (and the better half too) ; the contemplation of crime is respectable and praised by cabinet ministers and clergymen ; far more is known of, and far greater

A modern Balinese drawing in Chinese ink
of a Kris dance

interest taken in the doings of criminals than in those of the greatest of contemporary benefactors. Crime has the greatest fascination of all human activities (if it can be mixed with sex so much the better). Crowds will go to enormous trouble to look at the outside of a house in which violence has occurred, when not one of them will cross the street to visit the laboratory where discoveries which may influence their whole lives have been made. It would be impossible to imagine the unruly crowds which thronged to catch a glimpse of the coffin containing the body of poor Mrs. Rattenbury (who was acquitted of having helped her young lover murder her husband and then committed suicide), at the funeral of any notable or useful person.

This belief in the ecstasy of violence is at the root of our strongest modern mythologies. T. E. Lawrence worked with it, and Mussolini, taught by Sorel and Pareto, gave it theoretical and practical form. It is the emotional basis of all Fascist movements, which are based on consciously created mythologies (see Mussolini and Hitler *passim*). It is this ecstasy that feeling or using violence produces which holds together the Fascist movements, and which intoxicates its adherents, so that for the sake of violent sensation they will lead voluntarily miserable lives and offer themselves to ghastly death, glorying in war and labour and discipline. Fascism is for its followers in the last resort an anti-rational system founded on sensation, and continually more violent sensation;

de Sade has shown where such a system leads. It can only be combated by another mythology with equal appeal.

The Bolsheviks are also developing a mythology, but it is at present too Semitic, too black-and-white to be useful artistically ; it would be desirable if Communists could keep Christianity to be used as a mythology without intrinsic emotional values.

I think that for art to produce a type of life sufficiently interesting for all so that physical sensationalism shall not have too strong an appeal, and for it to be important for the majority (instead of as now for an insignificant minority), a mythology with its implied scale of values is absolutely necessary to provide common ground where the artist and his audience can meet. How we are to set about acquiring one I cannot imagine.

The cultivation of M.E. is a more complicated problem. Since it is for the greatest extent subjective its social value is questionable. Communities where it takes a preponderating place—West Africa or Thibet—are static and materially miserable. Communities where it is almost entirely neglected—the industrialised countries—seem spiritually unsatisfied. It undoubtedly gives the greatest possible selfish and subjective satisfaction of which man is capable, and, at second hand, seems to give sense and form to the life of the community. I think that it is possible that in a century or so it may be possible to investigate it thoroughly in the laboratory. The difficulty at present in the way is the question of emotion ; interest in other things is apparently fatal, which prevents scientists being their own experiment animals ; and people with a natural talent that way are usually either frightened of, or opposed to scientific investigation ; they wish to exploit the energy commercially— mediums, founders, and supporters of modern " magical " religions, such as Christian Science and Theosophy—or they regard the manifestations as oversignificant. I think possibly subjects might be found among prisoners ; I heard of one prison in California (I think, certainly in the Southern States) in which there was much solitary confinement, where the majority of prisoners indulged in the cultivation of M.E.—they called it " escaping," and had worked out the usual concentration technique—and found incidentally that they were able to hold telepathic conversations. Unfortunately my informant, an ex-prisoner, was somewhat drunk the only time I met him, and I could not get more details. I know that unless—or until—I go to prison, I shall never have the detachment necessary to try and see what happens.

It is only in the last three hundred years in Western Europe that M.E. has not been cultivated. In the Church it was apparently cultivated exclusively by the monastic orders, and not by the officiating clergy ; in the witch cult, until its destruction about 1600 by the whole community. I have an immense admiration for Margaret Murray's work, but I think she overemphasises the common-sense quality of the witch cult. Also I think she ought to investigate the illusions induced by bella donna. In many ways I believe that the study of the effects of intoxicating and anæsthetising drugs could give a good deal of information on the way M.E. works, for it would seem that the uniform disturbances produced by concentration have a certain amount in common with the uniform disturbances in the " higher centres" produced by drugs.

Finally, and this may be the most important, the Balinese are organised in what seems to be the optimum-size group—the large village community, in which everyone knows the other components of the group, but which is large enough for them to live privately. Their sense of belonging to a larger community is maintained by the annual pilgrimage, imposed on every Balinese, to the temple of Besaki, the holiest spot in the island. In this way too great a local patriotism is avoided.

It may be thought that a great deal of what I have written has little to do with Bali. In Bali I saw the only happy large community I have seen in my life, and I have tried to analyse for myself and others how this happiness is brought about and maintained, and have tried to apply my conclusions to the conditions around me. Perhaps more able people will re-do the task and reach more practical conclusions. For I do not want to think of the happiest community that I know half the world away in another hemisphere. I want it in the streets outside my door.

NOTE

In the above section I have used or referred to the following works :

Oudheden van Bali. By Dr. W. F. Stutterheim. (Published by the Kirthya Liefrinck-van der Tuuk association.)

Indian Influences on Old Balinese Art. By Dr. Stutterheim. (Published by the India Society.)

Bali. By G. Krause.

Bali. By P. J. van Baarda. (A Guide book.)

Varieties of Religious Experience. By William James.

Extrasensory Perception. By Dr. Rhine. (London : Faber and Faber.)

Wild Talents. By Charles Fort. (New York : Claude Kendall.)

Mystiques et Magiciens au Tibet. By Madame Alexandra David-Neel. (Paris : Plon et Cie. London : The Bodley Head. And also the other books by this author).

The Witch Cult in Western Europe, and *The God of the Witches.* By Margaret Murray. (London : Sampson Low.)

INTERLUDE. BATAVIA TO SAIGON

(i) BATAVIA TO SINGAPORE

IT WASN'T really a passenger boat at all. It was carrying a full cargo of rice and tobacco and tea to London and Amsterdam, travelling very leisurely ; and with that a few passengers as super-cargo. There were eight cabins forward, a small saloon and dining-room, and a tiny deck. For the journey to Europe it would be horribly confined, but for a couple of days it was pleasant enough. Considering the limited means at their disposal, the company looked after us nicely. With a restraint almost unparalleled among Dutch officers, nobody tried to make me play bridge at ten o'clock in the morning.

Besides ourselves there were three other passengers : a Scotsman, who was in charge of a tea plantation near Bandoeng, who was returning home on leave after five years ; a representative of some firm in Singapore, who was returning to his office after a short business trip ; and a third young man whose nationality and business appeared a complete mystery. His aloofness and refusal to speak to anybody was, on so small a boat, very marked ; for with our single common-room and tiny deck we were continually on top of one another. We had not been at sea many hours before the rest of us knew a good deal about one another. The Scotch tea-planter had a great deal of interest to tell ; his plantation was in the hills and fairly isolated, and the natives who worked for him were in a far earlier stage of development than the greater part of the Javanese. Though nominally Mohammedans their lives were chiefly regulated by " animistic " beliefs and practices ; the Scotsman told us of a number of peculiar rites which he had surprised or been invited to. He seemed to have considerable sympathy with his workers and spoke of them with affection ; two nights before, he had given them a feast to celebrate his departure and they had made him some presentation or other. I was sorry that I could not take notes of what he told us ; apart from the peculiar appearance of such behaviour I was feeling too lazy.

While the Scotsman had been talking, the unknown traveller had been sitting near us, reading one of the local papers ; but when the Scotsman started describing his different workers he got up and passed us and went to his cabin. If the sea had not been glassy smooth I should have said he was going to be sick. He was fairly tall, with brown hair, apparently in the middle twenties ; he was very pale and the skin was stretched tight over his cheek-bones ; he had rather handsome brown eyes, but there was a strained look about them, and they were never still. His very broad hands always looked clammy.

After that first afternoon we only saw him at mealtimes. The rest of the time he must have spent in his cabin. And even at meals he only bowed to the company and immediately propped some book or paper against the glass in front of him and pretended to read it ; at least it seemed as though it were pretence, for I never saw him turn over a page.

Naturally we talked about him. From one of the officers we learned that his name was Muller, and that he was travelling straight through to Amsterdam ; as far as the officer knew he would be the only passenger after Belawan Deli. The business man swore that he took opium : " Believe me, I've seen enough of them : I can always tell," but I didn't think he was right ; neither his complexion nor his eyes showed any of the usual stigmata. I thought he seemed frightened ; and I noticed that he repressed a shiver each time a Javanese boy handed him a dish.

On the second evening out I felt disinclined for sleep. My cabin was rather stuffy and the weather very warm ; there was a quarter moon in the sky and numberless stars, and instead of following the others to bed I stayed on deck. Except for the officers on the bridge the decks appeared quite empty ; so I decided to trespass and leave the passenger deck and explore the rest of the ship. After a good deal of clambering I arrived at the stern and leant over the taffrail, watching the ever-fascinating spectacle of the wake of the ship traced through the moon-dappled, oily waters. The movement of a ship at night and alone is for me always an awe-inspiring spectacle ; the lines where Sophocles, in the second chorus of the *Antigone*, places first among the wonders of man the fact that he ventures himself upon the colourless sea amidst wintry storms and the surging waves, have always a very personal appeal for me ; possibly the quietness gives a strange quality to a ship which the aeroplane never possesses. Half-hypnotised, I stared at the changeless movement of the water, when I was roused by a curious noise near me, almost a snort ; I looked round and saw that the mysterious Muller was engaged in the same occupation as myself, but a few yards away from me and in the shadow, so that I had not noticed him when I arrived. Tears were streaming down his face and glistening in the moonlight ; the snort which had aroused me was a strangled sob.

"What on earth is the matter ? " I asked, possibly indiscreetly ; but I was very frightened that in his despair he was contemplating suicide ; I did not like the idea of having to cope with such an emergency.

"Ich bin so furchtbar einsam," he replied, still crying.

My German has recently got fairly rusty, for I have had little occasion to use it, and I felt rather uncomfortable ; and anyhow if a complete stranger suddenly tells you, in no matter what language, that he is in despair because he is so horribly lonely, it

H

is difficult to know what to reply. It was on the tip of my tongue to tell him that if he treated everybody so cavalierly as he had treated us passengers he had only himself to thank. On the boat at any rate we had been perfectly willing to be friendly ; it was entirely his own action that had kept him apart. " But you are going home now to your people," I said.

" What people ? " he turned on me.

" Well, your family," I said. I thought I had started a consoling topic, only to be jumped on for an apparently tactless remark.

" I have no family," he said. " No family. Every month since I have been in this filthy place I have sent money home to my Mütterchen and now she has gone and married again a frightful chap. He is a rogue, a profiteer, ach ! unspeakable. Never will I speak to her again ! "

" Are you going back to Germany ? " I asked.

" I don't know ; I can't tell. What does it matter to you ? "

What indeed ? " I'm sorry," I said.

He turned round and looked at me full for the first time. He had stopped crying and his eyes looked like those of a dog which is frightened of receiving a beating. " Wissen Sie, ich bin ein diener," he said, defiantly. So that was where the trouble lay ; he was a " menial " and was ashamed of it, or ashamed of it being known. I'm afraid I was rather disappointed ; in such a setting the distress of occupying a slightly lower rung in the social scale than he thought he had a right to seemed to me slightly comic. And yet his distress was genuine enough.

I felt in rather an uncomfortable position. I had no desire to hear a hard-luck story which I felt I knew already ; on the other hand, to break off the conversation now would be unpardonable.

" Would you care for a drink ? " I asked. " I think there'll probably still be someone at the bar to serve us."

" No," he almost shouted. " I loathe being waited on, especially by those brutes of Javanese. Lord, how I loathe them ! The one reason why I'm going to Europe is to get away from these endless Asiatics. I suppose it's pleasant enough to come and look at them for a few weeks, but to live among them, ugh ! Listen. Did you go to the Zoo at Sourabaya and see the old orang-outan there ? The huge brute crouching in the corner with his arms round his knees, the little pig eyes looking ever so wisely at nothing out of that mask of a face ? That's the father of all Malays, I tell you. Out in the north of Sumatra there's an ape-man in the woods ; they don't know if it's a man or an ape, and they've passed a special bye-law forbidding people to shoot it, in case its human. It's a fact. I'm only surprised they're not more of them.

" Look at a Malay when he's not working. What's he doing ? I can tell you : nine times out of ten sitting down and *looking at nothing*. Not thinking, not talking, *looking at nothing !* It's not human, I tell you, it's like an animal, an ape. And for the last five years I've spent all my time with them when I've not been working myself. Man, it's enough to drive you mad. If you pay them and suggest something for them to do they're agreeable enough, but by themselves they just sit. They don't think. They don't talk. They drain the life out of you.

" Five years I've been out here, without a break. Not a single day without these brown faces round me all the time. Awake or asleep. I even dream of them now. I'm afraid of sleep because of my dreams. In Berlin I used to get to bed late enough, but when I slept I slept soundly.

" Do you know Berlin? One could have a good time there, eh? Man, when I think of the Resi., the Vaterland, all the places, the bars, the tanzdiele! In those days I used to get about. In the day I worked in the office of my uncle's hotel—it was by the Friedrichstrasse—and by night, man! did I have a good time. And there was a bit of money to pick up, too, if you knew how to set about it. That was what I called living. And then, when things started to go bad and the hotel business slumped, what should my fool of an uncle do but go and commit suicide! There was I without a job, or much chance of getting one. And my mother, with her little provision shop in Munich, had as much as she could do to make both ends meet. So there was I more or less on my beam ends. I picked up a sort of living round the bars and dancing places, taxi-dancer and so on.

You know. But that was no life for a man, and, anyhow, it was so uncertain.

" Among other things I used to show foreigners round the town. It's a good job when you can get it, your ten per cent from the places, as well as what your client gives you, and the free food and drink. I was fairly good at that. I could guess what people wanted and see that they got it, and I could make myself understood in English and Dutch. My clients used often to recommend me to their friends who were coming to the city to amuse themselves, and like that I'd usually got something to look forward to to carry me over the lean times.

" Well, one Dutchman sent another—I had a lot of Dutchmen—and at last a man called Jan came to me with an introduction. He was a rubber planter, home from the Indies on a few months' leave. He'd got money to burn—rubber was booming then—and we fairly painted the town red. Jan seemed a decent sort of bloke, and he took to me, in a nice sort of fatherly way ; said he didn't like to see a young man living the sort of life I did, and going on about the open air and so on, and ended up by offering me a place on his plantation. At the time I didn't take much to this suggestion—I didn't like the idea of living away from a big town—but I didn't turn it down altogether because it was always something to fall back on. When Jan went away he deposited the price of a passage out for me with a shipping agent. He wouldn't give me the money directly, for he

thought I'd spend it. He'd have been right, too,
For after he left I didn't earn anything worth while ;
things were going from bad to worse, places were
shutting up, there were no more foreigners, no more
money. I hung on for a bit, and then decided to try
the East. Things were looking too black at home ;
I couldn't be worse off. So I took up the passage and
then wrote to Jan that I was coming. I didn't give
him time to reply in case he'd changed his mind.

" When I got to Batavia I was practically penniless.
Jan didn't meet me, and I had to beg lifts to get to his
plantation the other side of the island. When I
arrived at last I found he had declared himself bank-
rupt. Just my luck. Rubber had fallen so that you
couldn't give it away, after its boom ; Jan hadn't
foreseen this, and had started making all sorts of
enlargements and improvements to his estate ; and
now he'd got no money to pay for them. So there
was I the other side of the world with no money and
no prospects. Jan gave me enough to get back to
Batavia and to live for a few days while I looked for a
job. And he gave me a lot of letters of introduction.

" After a time I got a job as barman and chucker-
out at a sort of night club run by Russians ; but that
didn't last long because the slump was hitting everyone and people had less money to spend. At the
beginning it was dreadful the way the money was
spilt ; planters used to come in from the country for
the week-end to have a good time, and they were
absolutely reckless. Sign piles of chits as high as the

bar ; break up the place for the fun of it and then sign
chits for the replacements ; drink two or three bottles
of genever apiece. They were louts, unrefined,
provincial, rude ; how I loathed them. They didn't
know how to enjoy themselves ; it was just throwing
money away. More often than not I was kept up till
dawn, and slept most of the day ; I'd got a room in a
sort of boarding-house and was putting money away—
I must say I got big tips—and sending some home
regularly. I learned Malay too, took lessons.

" But when things started to get slack I had more
time to myself, and then I knew what being lonely
meant. I hadn't a soul to speak to. People who'd
been as matey as you like when they were at the bar
cut me dead in the street, or else just nodded and went
on. People wouldn't have me to their house : I was
a foreigner, and then I was in a low job ; clerks don't
have barmen to the house. Not that I really wanted
to visit them, except to have someone to talk to ;
I like to talk and joke and say what's in my mind and
what's worrying me. And there wasn't a soul who'd
talk to me, sober.

" And then the Malays. I could get along with
them for work and that sort of thing, but I had no
desire to go beyond that. Of course I could go to bed
with the girls if I liked to pay, but I didn't care so
much about it, and anyhow, that didn't alter the
situation much. I didn't so much want people to go
to bed with, I wanted people to talk to.

" Well, in the end the bar shut up, and after a bit

I got a job in a hotel out in the country, in a smallish town. I already knew the work, and didn't mind it. I really had to run the hotel, look after the books, the catering, the bar, the visitors. It wasn't much work, for I'd plenty of Javanese and Chinese under me; but I had to look after everything; I was busy all the time, and except when visitors arrived or left I was all the time with Malays, coaxing them, ordering them about, keeping them in order. I practically never spoke to a white man or woman; the other white people in the place almost looked on me as a sort of Malay; and the Malays themselves almost looked on me as one of them. You see, at the hotel they saw me taking orders, or being told off by the guests if something didn't suit them. And then you can't be shouting at people all the time; you feel amiable sometimes and make a joke or pass a remark on the visitors or something; they called me Tuan, but they didn't respect me.

" When I had my day off I used to go out into the country, hunting or fishing; I used to pay the expenses so I always had as many people with me as I wanted. But I wanted somewhere to go in the evenings, and if a man doesn't have a woman at all he gets ill. I got a half-caste girl, Anna her name was, and kept her : she wasn't bad, though she was really just like the other Malays, only a little taller.

" Of course she considered herself a European— you know if any Javanese have white blood in their veins and pass certain exams, they are treated as

Dutchmen—but she wasn't even legally ; her father, whoever he was, had never acknowledged her and she'd been no good at school. She was always very bitter against her father, thought he'd done her an injury by not acknowledging her ; but the better-class Javanese didn't take to the half-caste, and because of her white blood she thought she was above the common rut. So she was nearly as lonely as I was. But not quite. She'd got her mother, and her mother's brother, her uncle, always with her ; and I soon found I was keeping them as well as her.

" I didn't mind that so much, for they didn't cost anything worth mentioning, but I did resent the way they had of treating me as if I was part of the family. The old mother was fat and dirty, and she used to come up to the hotel with messages for her ' son-in-law ' until I made the hell of a row ; it made me look like dirt. And the uncle was a thoroughly disreputable old fellow, who made a living by doctoring the sillier natives and giving them amulets and love philtres and things. I thought he was an old rogue and let him see it.

" Well, things went on all right for a couple of years, until Anna said she was going to have a baby, and that I must marry her so that her child shouldn't suffer under the same disadvantages as she had. Of course I told her not to be silly, that the idea was simply absurd ; I said I'd acknowledge the child, so that its legal existence would be all right, and that I'd help her with the expense and so on ; in fact I made far more generous offers than most people would do in such a case ; but she wouldn't be satis-fied ; she wanted marriage, and nothing else. It was an absolute obsession with her. Her child would be almost white, she said ; it must live the life of a white man, and not start as a bastard. There were endless scenes. In the end I stopped going to her house any more, so as to have a little peace.

" That made matters worse, for she started coming to the hotel and made scenes there. In the end I had to go to the police and get an order made out for-bidding her to come there, on pain of punishment. She made me absurd, and upset the guests. I tried to find another job elsewhere through advertisements, but there aren't many jobs going now.

" After the threat from the police Anna kept quiet, and I didn't see anything of her, but I began to be haunted by that old villain her uncle. Whenever I went out I seemed to see him. One day he followed me into the Chinese barber's shop, and picked up a bit of my cut hair before the barber chased him out. ' They try and get hair so as to make magic,' he explained to me. ' They are all heathens.'

" Another day, after a shower, the old man appeared in front of the hotel and scraped up the imprint of my footstep in the mud. Of course all the boys at the hotel knew who he was, and the whole story, and one of the waiters came and begged me, when he saw what the old man was doing, to leave the neighbourhood before the spell could be made, and when I refused, tried to tell me of a rival magician who could render useless in advance whatever mischief the old man might be contemplating. Of course I couldn't do a thing like that; everybody would know about it, and my position would become impossible. And, anyhow, I didn't believe he could do anything unless perhaps poison me; and I took good care not to eat anything which I hadn't seen others already eat. Besides, after that wet day I didn't see the old man again.

" People say that when you live all your time with natives, and that's really what I was doing, you begin to think like them. Well, it's not true. The more I saw of the Malays, the better I got to know them, the more alien they seemed to me. They seem like humans when you don't know them well; they're not really.

" Well, things went on more or less as usual. On my afternoons off I went into the country, and the evenings I spent in my room. I heard and saw nothing of Anna or her uncle, and more or less forgot about them. Then one day I got a letter from Anna, nicely written and very calm; she apologised for all the fuss she had made, and said she realised now that she had been unreasonable; she was near her time and wanted to see me again before the baby was born. Would I go and see her my next free evening?

" First of all I decided I wouldn't, and then I thought, why not? After all, she was the only living person with whom I had any sort of emotional contact at all—for I had just heard of my mother's second marriage. And Malay for Malay, she was as good as another. And I wanted to be able to see the baby after it was born—I don't know why. So I went.

"Anna and her mother were as nice to me as they knew how, and made me feel a fool. They'd prepared a very special rijstaffel for me ; and I took great care not to eat anything which I didn't see them eat first. But after dinner Anna started the old story again, first of all trying to cajole me into marrying her with all the silly blandishments she could ; and when that was no good, she started making vague threats. I wasn't going to stand that, so I got up and went towards the door to go away. She threw herself on the ground in front of me and caught hold of my knees, saying I shouldn't leave till I promised to marry her. I tried to make her leave go, gently because of the baby, but she clung harder still and I told her if she didn't leave go I'd make her. 'Very well,' she said, 'I'll let you go on one condition ; tell me one reason why you won't marry me. You must like me or you wouldn't have stayed with me two years ; I can cook well, I can look after your house better than a white woman ; I'm going to have your baby. Why won't you marry me ? ' 'If you want to know,' I said, 'it's because you're a Malay, and I don't want to spend the rest of my days with any one of your colour.' It was a bit brutal, but I was thoroughly worked up. 'You don't like my colour,' she said. 'Not good enough for you, I suppose ? ' I'd not meant that, I merely meant that Malays weren't the same sort of persons as we are, but it wasn't worth while explaining. 'Well, I'll tell you one thing,' she went on, almost shrieking, ' you won't marry anybody else who looks a different colour, you won't see anybody who looks a different colour ! ' and then she suddenly bit my hand as hard as she could. Her teeth almost met. I pushed her aside then, and hurried back to the hotel. I swabbed my hand with iodine before I went to bed.

" I'd not been at the desk long the next morning before Anna walked up to it, as calm as you please. Naturally, I jumped at her. ' What do you mean by coming here ! ' I shouted. ' Get out before I call the police.' ' Goodness ! the man's gone mad,' Anna said, and she said it in English ; but Anna didn't know a word of English, just Javanese and a few Dutch phrases. And then Anna turned and called : ' John ! come here at once ! ' and I swear her old uncle came up. ' Look here, what's the meaning of this ? ' he said. ' What do you mean by frightening my wife ? '

" I recognised his voice, for he and his wife, a couple of English tourists, had been stopping at the hotel some days ; but when I looked at them, there was Anna and her uncle. I made some apology about not feeling well, and the sun, and went away to see about the orders for the day. I thought I must have had some sort of daydream, for the Javanese and Chinese were just the same as usual, but when I went

into the dining-room at lunch-time every table was
occupied by Annas and her uncles. Every white
woman I saw looked like Anna, every white man like
her uncle. It was horrible, and what was worse, I
couldn't do my work properly any more ; when all
the clients looked the same I never knew which were
speaking to me.

" I went to the Dutch doctor, but even after I'd
made him believe me he couldn't do anything ; he
made me wear dark glasses, but that didn't make
any difference. Of course the servants at the hotel
noticed soon enough what was wrong with me, at
least not exactly, but they more or less guessed. They
helped me as much as they could by describing the
clients when they came to ask me something. The
waiter who'd advised me to go to another magician
before, kept on coming and asking me to go with him
to be cured, but I wouldn't at first ; I didn't want to
admit to myself that I'd been bewitched. And,
anyhow, if I'd disliked the Malays before, I loathed
them now ; I didn't want to have anything to do
with them. But it went on just the same, Anna and
her uncle everywhere, till I felt I was going crazy ;
and at last I went with the waiter to his old sorcerer.

" Not that it did much good. After I'd screwed
myself up to tell him the story, he hummed and
hawed and said the best thing was to marry the girl,
as that would stop it at once : but I'd sooner have
died than do that. Then he said the next best thing
was to get some of her hair, and nail-parings, and

blood so as to make another spell which would make her so uncomfortable that she'd take off mine. But we're in the twentieth century; I can't go about picking up other people's nail-clippings, even if she'd give me the chance, which wasn't likely; and apparently it wasn't any good if anyone else did it. So the magician said he couldn't help me. But as I was going away he added : ' It won't travel over water.'

" Well, I stood it as long as I could, but in the end I gave up. My life wasn't worth living. I resigned my job and now I'm on my way back home. If half the world between us won't stop it, there are doctors in Europe, psychoanalysts, I don't know."

" Why ? " I asked. " Is it still the same ? Do we still all look like Anna or her uncle ? "

" You all did the first day, and I've not dared look at anyone since."

" You looked at me earlier this evening," I said.

" Yes," he replied, " but you were against the light ; I couldn't make out your features at all."

I didn't reply, but lit a match so that the flare lit up both our faces. After that I went back to my cabin, for the expression on his face showed clearly enough how mine had appeared to him.

We got into Singapore at dawn the next morning.

INTERLUDE. BATAVIA TO SAIGON

(ii) SINGAPORE TO SAIGON

AT SINGAPORE we changed on to a French boat, and I must admit it was a great relief. The Dutch are (doubtless) paragons of all the solider virtues, but they have little taste for the minor pleasures of life. After the dowdy heaviness of Dutch furniture and decoration the boat appeared to be designed with the greatest elegance. It was a pleasure to lie down on a mattress instead of the hygienic boards which cover the Dutch East Indies ; and to eat civilised food again was an ecstasy. For those who have not a passion for rather tough, over-cooked beef, prepared in various ways, meals in the Dutch Indies are a nightmare ; for no Dutchman, apparently, considers he has had a solid meal unless there have been at least three meat courses in its composition. There is no reason why this Dutch colonial food should be so unpleasant, for in French Indo-China, which has less natural advantages, one can eat as well as in France, or very nearly ; but the Dutch despise all vegetarian or fish or egg dishes ; beef, rissoles, and hotpot should be the centre of every meal. The only break in this procession of dead cows is an occasional rijstaffel ; this is a curry in which all the ingredients, instead of being served already mixed as in Indian curries, are handed separately, a big dish of each meat or vegetable prepared in its own sauce. This gives the impression of an enormous meal, for there are more than a dozen boys (in the big hotels) handing dishes ; actually one does not eat more than with an ordinary curry. As a change of diet this rijstaffel is quite pleasant ; I found on the whole that the smaller the place at which it was served the better it was cooked. At one or two rest-houses it was excellent ; at the big and pretentious Javanese hotels rather nasty.

The boat was practically empty ; it had dropped most of its passengers at Singapore. The hot weather was starting in Indo-China, and there were only a few tourists like ourselves on board. For the return journey, on the other hand, the boat was already over-crowded, and cables demanding accommodation were arriving all the time ; everybody who possibly could was going home on leave.

The boat contained a handsome and spacious bar, rather prettily decorated with reproductions of the frescoes of Knossos ; and inevitably in the evening I found my way there. In one corner a party of Americans were playing bridge with the hushed expression people reserve for funerals, *faux pas*, and the forcing club ; from time to time one of them would look round at the hilarious party the other side of the room, glaring at them as though they were

I

brawling in church. The party certainly was rather
noisy ; five people were giving the impression of a
large crowd. The central figure in this party was a
rather plump French woman, certainly the wrong side
of forty ; she was dressed in an elaborate black evening
dress and wore a number of diamonds ; she had
an almost theatrical make-up which contrasted rather
oddly with her obviously uncontrollable dyed bobbed
hair. She had a very penetrating voice and an infec-
tious laugh ; everything she said carried to the
farthest corner of the room, and occasionally if one
of her companions made a good remark she would
repeat it for the benefit of the barman, with whom she
seemed on very friendly terms. The rest of her party
consisted entirely of men ; seated beside her on the
bench was a man who was just not young enough to
be her son ; he was tall and pale, with black hair,
rather good-looking ; he was the quietest of the party.
He was dressed in rather too well made and too new
a dinner jacket, and on the whole spoke very little ;
he seemed rather uncomfortable in his clothes, and he
was obviously so muscular that they seemed misplaced
on him ; the tattooing which showed on his wrists
looked oddly incongruous against the white starched
cuffs with the diamond and enamel links. The rest
of the party consisted of two of the ship's officers and
a very upright, elderly, white-haired man. This last
man seemed to me vaguely familiar ; I thought I
remembered his face, or rather the network of
wrinkles which covered it ; for I have unfortunately a

frightfully bad memory for people ; I will seize on one characteristic—the voice, the way the hair grows, pigmentation, perhaps even the clothes—of people I meet, and remember that while I completely forget whom such a characteristic belongs to. I was sure I had seen that man's wrinkles somewhere before ; but where and in what circumstances I could not tell. Perhaps I had merely sat opposite him for some time.

I must have looked at him a good deal, trying to wrack my memory as to where I had seen him before, for he kept on turning round and looking at me, with a sort of half-smile of recognition ; eventually he came over to me and said : " How do you do ? What a surprise seeing you here."

I returned his greeting, but I was just as much in the dark as to who he was, and was quite at a loss what to say next. I think my embarrassment must have shown, for the stranger helped me out by asking : " How did you like Morocco when you got there ? "

With that hint I remembered him completely. I had met him about eighteen months earlier on a boat going from Bordeaux to Casablanca ; the weather had been very rough and in the evenings we had been practically the only passengers about. I am not a particularly good sailor, but with a sufficient supply of brandy and sugar I can keep upright in most weathers. We had talked a good deal on this boat, Palloni—yes, that was his name—and I ; he had an endless stock of conversation and anecdote. He was a Corsican by birth, and by profession was, or had been, almost everything. He had two separate aims in Morocco, which fairly well indicated the diversity of his interests ; he was going to investigate, quite unofficially, the petroleum wells which had been discovered in the Atlas mountains, but which for some reason were not going to be exploited ; and he was also going to try to collect a troup of Moroccan jugglers and Schleu dancers for some international exhibition somewhere or other. He appeared to be equally at home in the theatrical, the financial, and the political world ; he always seemed to have met the best-known figures of the day at moments in their lives when they did not want to be met by anybody ; he knew the background of every spectacular action or scandal ; in fact he was a walking— and talking—chronique scandaleuse. I didn't believe all he told me, but some of his more improbable stories I heard repeated later from the most trustworthy sources. I was glad to see him again for he was a most entertaining companion.

After a little conversation about Morocco, and after we had told one another why we were both on the boat—his reasons were as fantastic as usual, but discretion forbids me repeating them—I asked him to join me in a drink. " I'd like to later," he said ; " I must get back to my friends now. But I expect Rosel will go to bed early ; she's on her honeymoon."

" Rosel ? " I asked. " That's not the singer Rosel ? "

" You've heard her ? " he asked.

" Yes," I said. " About four years ago in a little

music-hall in the rue le la Gaîté. I went three nights running. She's the most extraordinary turn I've ever seen in my life."

The little popular theatres behind the Montparnasse station are occasionally quite amusing to go to in the evening in Paris, if there's nothing better to do. One night in the summer of 1930 I had dropped into one with a friend. The greater part of the programme had been fairly ordinary—the usual chansonniers making the usual jokes about the usual characters—and fairly dull dance turns. Towards the end of the programme " Rosel, chanteuse réeliste " was announced. The curtain went up on the usual curtain-draped stage, and a middle-aged woman in a rather shabby black dress came in. She was fairly short and fat, with black hair, streaked with grey ; except for the blue round her eyes she was very little made up. She walked forward to the footlights and looked slowly round the audience. Everybody stopped fidgeting ; cigarettes were allowed to go out. The place felt cold. I have never seen such a look of deadly hatred in any eyes as the look this Rosel directed at the anonymous audience. It was frightening.

Then she started to sing. Her voice had a slight rasping quality, but was otherwise in no way peculiar. Where she got her songs from I don't know, for I have never heard any others like them. The tunes were commonplace enough—some indeed were well known—but the words were extraordinary. They were drab and cynical songs about street-walkers in the rain, coming back without money, and being knocked about by their ponces ; about an old woman who hated everybody she saw because she was neglected ; about a girl who took cocaine, until she went mad. The songs seemed completely misplaced in a popular music-hall, suited rather to some very intellectual soirée—no, you would have said they were unsingable. But Rosel held the rough audience motionless ; as she sang she lived the miserable and degraded stories she told, lived them with an intensity which was painful ; and besides making these characters vivid she somehow conveyed to the audience the message that they were responsible for the degradation they were witnessing. It's very difficult to convey the quality of her performance ; it was realism and satire and accusation all mixed together. I got the impression that she had no wish at all to please the audience ; she wanted to startle them, to shock them out of their complacency. When the curtain went down on her turn there was a moment's complete silence, and then uproarious applause. For a long time she wouldn't give an encore, and when she did she sang a popular song of the day, a rather sentimental melody ; she sang it without expression, listlessly, so that all the shoddiness, all the false sentimentality, all the glittering dustiness of the world the song came from stood out naked. I was so moved that I would not wait for the rest of the programme.

I returned the next night, and the night after,

trying to find out where her power lay. I didn't discover much. She seemed to live the life of her songs, so that she filled the stage with ghosts ; as the street-walker minced along the rainy streets, stopping at the corners with a smile that was meant to be alluring but was half despair and half fear, you forgot the airless theatre. But it was the bitterness, the palpable hatred, that I wanted to analyse ; and that I was quite unable to do.

I had never seen her perform again. I frequently saw her name on the bill-boards, and learned that she was becoming a popular star ; but after the pound left gold Paris became too expensive for a prolonged stay, and on the occasions when I was there she was either not appearing or I had no free evening. I remembered every detail of her performance with the greatest vividness.

When Palloni told me that the lively and rather outrageous lady opposite was Rosel, I looked at her more closely to try to trace some resemblance with the singer who had made so strong an impression on me. It was physically possible for them to be the same woman, but never in a thousand years would I have guessed her identity.

" You better come and make her acquaintance," Palloni said. " Her name's Madame Riquet ; that's her husband beside her."

On the whole I dislike meeting people I admire, dislike even meeting celebrities ; it is almost always a disappointment. But Rosel, apparently guessing

what Palloni had said, shouted out across the room :
" Bring your friend over."

When I was introduced to Rosel I tried to tell her
how much I admired her performance, but I stam-
mered rather over it, for I am always very clumsy
at such sort of pretty speeches ; and she cut me
short with : " Take it as said ; sit down and have a
glass of bubbly," then, turning to her husband,
added : " Order another bottle, Jean darling."

Jean Riquet gave the order with a most distinguished
air, but he had a Parigot accent which you could cut
with a knife. The accent of the Parisian faubourgs is
even more marked than cockney ; it is rather pretty,
but it has a slightly sinister undertone, a threat
instead of a whine. I was rather taken aback, for
almost certainly the first class of a French boat had
never heard such a voice before. Parigot is far less
common than cockney, and is almost entirely confined
to unskilled workers and apaches ; except round the
big markets and by the boulevards extérieurs you
practically never hear it.

I did not fit very well into the party I had joined.
It was almost too lively for my taste. Rosel was quite
half-tipsy, and she was determined that everything
anybody said or did should be funny and, if possible,
obscene ; she was very witty at times, but quite
outrageous ; even the ship's officers looked slightly
uncomfortable and glanced round from time to time
to see if anybody was overhearing, and, if overhearing,
was shocked. There was nobody very near.

At eleven o'clock Rosel said to her husband : " Sign for what we've had, darling ; time we were all in bed. I won't say asleep, for that wouldn't suit me at all. After all, a girl only has a honeymoon once." She and her husband went away, and the officers left shortly after. I reminded Palloni of his promise to have a drink with me, and we settled down comfortably in a corner.

After we had talked of different subjects for some time Palloni said : " It's difficult to realise now that Rosel was once the chief rival of Régine Flory and Gaby Deslys, that she was once the 'toast of the boulevards,' as they say."

I was astounded. " You don't mean it," I said.

" She was a big star before the war," he replied. " She was a delicious little thing, the daintiest dancer, like thistledown. And then she'd got a sort of spring-time freshness, an innocence which was absolutely enchanting. At least that's how we saw it at the time ; there was a great vogue for spring-time freshness then. Not that she had much talent : but she had enormous charm."

" You're joking," I said. " Why, when I first saw her four years ago nobody had heard her name ; and as for charm—well ! "

" You saw her when she was making her come-back she left the stage for fifteen years."

" Did she marry then ? " I asked.

" No, this is the first time she's been married. It's a stranger story than that. I'll tell you if you like ; you might be able to make a play out of it.

" As I told you, from about 1910 Rosel was one of
the first stars of the Parisian musical comedy stage.
She became a star almost in a night ; one day nobody
had heard of her, and the next day people talked about
nobody else.   She got a small part in a revue—a
couple of songs and dances—and all Paris flocked to
see her.   After her last appearance the house half
emptied.   She became the rage of the season.   Everybody wanted to take her out, to be seen about with
her.   You know that's how things are in Paris ; some
girl or other becomes the fashion, and every man who
enjoys that sort of publicity—and that means most
Frenchmen—wants to be seen in public with her.
Nothing more than that ; they pretend they want to
become the girl's lover, but they don't really ; if
they were offered the choice of either being the girl's
lover secretly or being falsely reputed to be her lover
they would all of them choose the latter.   When a
girl becomes the rage like that she can make her
fortune if she's clever ; but most of them don't ;
they lose their heads.

" Rosel was one of the clever ones.   Where she came
from nobody knew—it was said she was born in the old
port of Marseilles—but she knew exactly how to
behave on every occasion.   I said there seemed
something virginal about her, and there was ; she
took everything she could from everyone, but she didn't
give anything.   She was ' given her establishment '
by a senator, a retired and extremely rich manu-
facturer, in the good old-fashioned way : but the

senator was so extremely old that—well, she seemed just as virginal as ever, and there was no reason to suspect otherwise.

" By the end of her first season she was established as a Parisian figure—one of the people who would inevitably be present at any fashionable resort, or race meeting, or night club. Naturally she became a star in her own right, and for three years running she had musical comedies specially written for her. She was established, and there seemed no reason why she should not continue for another forty years, exactly like all the other successful Parisiennes. She had a reputation which would have long outlasted her beauty. And then in the spring of 1914 she just disappeared. People talked about her a great deal, innumerable rumours were spread, and then she was forgotten. When she made her return in 1929 nobody remembered her ; some critics thought she had taken the name of an old star for the sake of the possible publicity. Not that she got any for it. The generation which had known Rosel was dead ; and the few who remembered her could see no connection between their memory and the woman in front of them. She was not even a ghost."

" And is nothing known," I asked, since he seemed to invite a comment, " of what had happened in those fifteen years ? Is there anything to prove she is the same person ? "

" There's no doubt about that," he replied. " She's proved it a hundred times, remembering people and places. And I know more or less what happened while she was away from France, though of course I don't know all the details.

" In 1914 Rosel fell in love. I've called her virginal several times, and if not technically correct it is an accurate psychological description. The idea of sex, of love, had no meaning for her. And she was so surrounded with all the signs of it that she must either have believed herself an anomaly or thought the rest of the world actors putting up a silly pretence. She didn't believe in love. And then she fell madly in love with a dancer who was her partner in her last musical show. She fell in love, abjectly, completely, body and soul as they say. It was like a madness for her, an obsession. She gave up everything and everybody for this man. In the middle of the run of her show she gave up her part, and made the man give up his ; she was so jealous that she could not bear to see him dancing and chatting with the other women in the cast. She took him away, out of Europe, always travelling on so that she should be alone with him ; they ended up in Shanghai.

" I must say I feel rather sorry for the man. It must be rather frightening to be swamped with such a fierce and jealous love. For there doesn't seem any reason at all to suppose he cared about her. As far as I can find out he was the usual type of gigolo-stage-dancer, good-looking, stupid, no more honest than he had to be. I never have been able to understand what women fall in love with, and I can't explain at all why Rosel picked on this one rather than the dozens of others who were exactly like him.

" After a time he began to resent the way Rosel was treating him. He was living in greater luxury than he had ever before in his life, he had everything he could wish for almost before he could formulate the wish, but with all that he had less freedom or independence than a pet pekingese. He couldn't speak to anybody, he couldn't go out for an hour alone without having a terrific scene when he came back. Rosel was madly in love with him, and she treated him like a slave. After a time he started to revolt against it, and told Rosel he was going back home. He acted as if he meant it too. She was terrified, and started giving him bigger and bigger presents to keep him with her. He found himself richer than he had ever been in his life, and with this comparative wealth he grew greedy. He wanted more, and to get it he started knocking Rosel about in the traditional way. And in the traditional way she gave him all he asked for, until she was almost literally penniless.

" And then, when he had got everything he could lay hands on, he cleared out, taking even her jewellery with him. He had no desire to go to the war, and Shanghai, with its French reservation, was none too safe a place for a man of military age. So one night he just disappeared ; I don't know what happened to him after.

" Rosel nearly went out of her mind with grief and

anxiety ; she was alone, penniless, and in a strange country. She caught typhoid, which probably saved her reason. She was in hospital for nearly a year. When she came out she looked more or less as you see her now ; her looks, her youthfulness, her charm had all gone. It was almost impossible for her to get back to France—this was in 1916—without money or friends or influence. I don't know if she made the effort. I've not been able to find out much about her life at Shanghai. She was filled with a bitter hatred against the whole world. She was almost intolerably miserable. She learned to make her misery bearable with cocaine and opium. To get money to buy the drugs she used to walk the streets by the port, waiting for sailors."

" Poor woman," I said. " So that's where she got her songs from."

"Yes," said Palloni. "She more or less made them up herself, and got them put into shape by professionals."

" And yet," I said, " it doesn't really explain much. Hundreds of others must have had experiences as painful as hers and have not been able to communicate them. I assure you her performance affected me physically ; it made me feel cold."

" I think you exaggerate," said Palloni. " But there was certainly a strange quality in her act. She wanted to make the world realise what it had done to her, she wanted to get her own back."

" How did she get back to Paris ? " I asked.

" Jean Riquet brought her back," he said.

" What ! that gangster ? "

" It's funny, isn't it ? But he's not a gangster, though he talks like one. Of course the accent gives him away at once—Place de la Bastille. And he can't get rid of it. He's taken enough lessons, but he's tone deaf. You didn't like him ? "

" He seemed to me fairly negative."

" And yet Rosel's success to-day, all that she has, all that she is, even being alive she owes to him. Riquet's a Parisian street arab, his voice told you that. I don't suppose even his mother knew who his father was. He was brought up on the streets and apprenticed to an electrical engineer when he was fourteen. He did very well at his job. He was serious, and quiet, and for his *milieu* very honest. Soon after he'd finished his military service he was sent out by his firm to supervise a job they were doing in Shanghai. One evening Rosel picked him up. He went home with her, and then for some reason she told him her story. I expect she was doped, she was most of the time. Anyhow, from that evening Riquet took charge of her. Although his position was quite good he wasn't earning very much money, but he managed to pay for her to be taken into the hospital there and to be de-intoxicated. It was a long business and before she was ready to come out Riquet's job was finished. All the same he waited for her ; after a great deal of difficulty he got her a passport—of course she'd lost hers years before—and brought her back with him to France, travelling steerage, naturally."

" One minute," I interrupted. " Do you mean he
was in love with her ? "

" I don't think so," said Palloni, " in fact I'm almost
sure not. I don't think he's in love with her now. It's
something much more complicated and much more
difficult to define than love. And of course he can't
analyse his sentiments. He once said that as soon as
he met her he felt that he had to look after her, to
re-establish her ; he didn't know why, but he knew
he had to do it. And I think we have to leave it like
that. You can talk about an Œdipus complex if
you like, but I don't think that makes things any
simpler. He must have needed endless patience, for
she was still as bitter as ever, and not in the least
grateful for all Riquet had done for her.

" When they got back to France Riquet found that
his job had been given to somebody else, because he
hadn't returned when he should have ; and it wasn't
too good a period for finding work. They lived for a
time on Riquet's savings, but they didn't last long, and
when he found that he couldn't get another job he said
that she would have to go back on the stage if they
weren't both to starve. First of all she wouldn't hear
of it ; she didn't believe that she could if she wanted
to, and anyhow, she was never going to do anything
to please or amuse people again. She hated everybody,
and if she had to die she couldn't hide her hate. And
then Riquet got the idea of dramatising this feeling of
hers. He persuaded and bullied her until she wrote
down the ideas for half a dozen songs which would

convey more or less what she wanted. Somehow or other he found people with the necessary skill to put the songs into proper shape and set them to music, and then they tried to get an engagement. Most of the impresarios laughed in her face when she asked for a job—an unknown middle-aged woman with grey hair !—and wouldn't even give her an audition ; they either had never heard of her before or didn't believe she was the Rosel they knew of. At last they found a small music-hall up in Montmartre whose proprietor had been a stage hand when Rosel was a star ; out of sentiment he gave her a week's engagement, though he paid her practically nothing.

" For the first performance Riquet filled the house with his friends, but it was quite unnecessary ; you know how she held the audience. She stayed at that music-hall for a month, and since then, if she's been without work it's been her own fault. She commands as big a salary as any actress in France."

" And she and Riquet have only just been married ? "

" Yes, when she started being a success he wanted to leave her. He felt that he'd done all his duty. I tell you, he's never been in love with her. And he didn't want to live on her. With the onset of the slump it was difficult to get a job, and when Riquet was offered one in Toulouse he accepted. First of all, Rosel was furious—she thought Riquet was abandoning her as the other had done—and then heart-broken ; she had become so used to Riquet that she couldn't

K

live without him.   She followed him to Toulouse, and
after long explanations she persuaded him to return
as her manager ;   and then a little while ago she
married him.   They're on their way back to Shanghai
for their honeymoon."

"If I'd not seen her on the stage," I said, "I should
never be able to believe you ; meeting her to-night
I thought her a rather coarse, jolly woman, without
a bother in the world, who'd bought herself a gigolo."

"I know," said Palloni.   "It's a change, isn't it ?
When she began to be a success and people started
running after her again, she became much less bitter ;
and Riquet has made her completely forget her first
lover.   I should say now she's as happy a woman as
you could meet.   Now don't you think that would
make a good play—suspense, drama, a happy
ending ? "

"No," I said.   "It wouldn't do.   Nobody else
could convey what she did with her singing ; and
then the story's not very probable, is it ? "

Although I didn't think I could make a play out of
Rosel's story I was very interested in her, and when a
few months after I returned to Europe I saw her billed
as the chief attraction at one of the Paris music-halls,
I made a point of going to see her act.   I noticed

Riquet in one of the boxes. As the chief star of the evening she was given the full stage, with a white-painted piano and lots of imitation flowers against " modernistic " curtains. She came on to the stage in an elaborate sequined evening gown, resplendent with diamonds, and carrying an ostrich-feather fan. She was greeted with a burst of applause, which she replied to with many smiles and bows, with a special glance towards Riquet. She sang a number of songs, some of them rather dirty, some of them sentimental ; a number of them were from American films. She sang with considerable gusto, and her jolly gaiety pleased the audience, who would not let her go. The friend I was with turned to me and said : " Can you tell me what all the fuss is about ? She seems to be nothing more than a rather second-rate Sophie Tucker ; she's got an agreeable personality, but she doesn't seem to me to have any talent at all." I couldn't find anything to say in reply.

PART TWO

THE ROAD TO ANGKOR

INDO-CHINA

ALL THAT I saw of French Indo-China—Cochin China and Cambodia—seemed to me to be completely uncalled for.

Saigon, the port and capital of the whole colony, is one of the greatest achievements of colonial construction, so they say, in the whole world. Less than a century ago the ground on which the city now stands was a swampy marsh a mere six feet above sea level. Now it is as solid and ugly as any small provincial French town you like to mention, with a coquettish little opry house with a pseudo-classical façade covered with angels and things, with big stores with plate-glass windows, with cafés on the side-walks, with an enormous governor's palace like a small Versailles, with lots of Government buildings, with a sport-club, with a dusty park containing a few miserable animals in tiny cages. Alongside all this solid respectability goes a viciousness which equals if it does not surpass the old port of Marseilles, or Cairo, or Suez. Every rickshaw boy, and there must be thousands of them, is a pimp : " Madame français, missou ? Madame métisse ? Madame annamite ? Boy français ? Boy

métisse ? Boy annamite ? Fumer ? Moi connais
bon." This might be their street cry : who'll buy
my sweet lavender ? The whole place and most of
the inhabitants have the sweet and acrid smell of
opium hanging around them. As far as I could see
there was nothing genuine, nothing spontaneous,
nothing that was not wholly commercial in the whole
town. I personally prefer a nice swampy marsh.

Dear Stella Benson, writing from considerable
experience, says flatly that the drive from Saigon to
Phnom Penh is the dullest day's work in the world.
"Saigon, as I see it, is not worth going to and,
equally, not worth coming away from." I think she
is right, too. Parts of Senegal and the French Soudan,
or the journey down the Volga, seem nearly as dull,
because they go on so much longer, but I question
whether even there you could find a five hours' drive
so completely void of any interest. For since Stella
Benson was there the road has been greatly improved,
and the journey only takes half a day ; I think,
however, the cars are still the same. I have never
seen, much less travelled in, such a collection of old
crocks. I am told that there is one car in the colony
which is not tied together with bits of string, which
has actually got treads on its tyres, which has got
uncracked mica and glass ; this mythical vehicle is
said to belong to the Governor-General ; but I did
not meet anybody who had seen it. The chief reason
for this, apart from parsimony, is the fact that the
piastre has been given the fixed value of ten francs

The Royal Palace
at Phnom Penh

for questions of international payments ; its internal purchasing power is less than half that amount.

There is one consolation ; anything with wheels which go round can, in time, negiotiate the journey from Saigon to Angkor. The road, and the surrounding countryside, are as flat as a calm sea, dirty yellow in colour, and with as little by the wayside to interest. If the road makes an angle of more than ten degrees large signs announce the *Virage* a mile away, in the hope that one of the passengers will be awake and will prod the chauffeur. This does not happen often ; perhaps a dozen times between Saigon and Phnom Penh. Phnom Penh—Penh of the Mountain—is the capital of modern Cambodia. In the midst of the town is a stupendous hill, rising a good fifty yards above sea level and the surrounding country ; this is the most important eminence for miles around, the hub of the kingdom, the landmark of the neighbourhood. It is a nasty little wart, covered with unconnected bits of masonry, small temples and tombs and ugly statues and empty animals' cages ; the top is surrounded by a stûpa, an ugly bell-shaped monument in grey stone erected to somebody's memory, which is lit up at nights with fairy lights in different colours.

The town is the usual colonial mixture of spacious European quarters, and crowded and filthy native slums ; it contains, besides two or three not unpleasant Buddhist temples, the palace of the present Emperor, where with considerable ingenuity is combined all that both Europe and Asia can offer of tawdry, gimcrack, flashy and pretentious bad taste. It is so ghastly that it has a sort of morbid fascination.

The architectural principle is " put a little bit on to the corner." Whenever a gable or a roof-end or a spire or anything like that occurs a crimped piece of metal is stuck on to it, contradicting the general lines so that every sky-line bristles with artificial flames, or the detached whiskers of Brobdingnagian prawns. The horror continues in the interior ; there is a royal chapel, filled with ikons and idols (Buddhist), whose ugliness is only equalled by the value of the materials employed ; there is a museum of the emperor's treasures, summed up in the billycock hat with a sun-burst of diamonds stuck into the centre of the crown. The only thing in the whole palace of any real charm is the sacred white elephant. My Lord Bishop is a most engaging animal, not at all white but rather a light beige ; he wears his holiness easily, and is very friendly, even frolicsome ; you can see he has a very nice nature, and for a few bananas is happy to make you joy and wreathe his lithe proboscis.

From Phnom Penh to Siemréap, the town of Angkor, is another day's dull drive, without incident or interest. Siemréap itself is a charming little village, hardly touched by European influence, built along a winding river ; the native houses are insignificant little structures in wood, hidden behind the vegetation which grows so lushly, and with so fresh a green along the river banks—bananas and bamboos, and the pink and white lotus, and various reeds, and a few larger trees ; here and there a house on stilts, to guard against the floods, and a water- or wind-mill. Here alone in all the Cambodia I saw are the eyes rested.

And the Cambodians ? An ugly, dull-looking people, diseased and under-nourished, cowed and frightened, drably dressed in dingy black ; with Buddha as their god, and opium as the way to Him. When I saw the Cambodian dancers at the Colonial Exhibition in Paris, I was very impressed with them ; I still think their " lifting " movement on one bent leg so that the whole body seems to be raised into the air very impressive ; but their whole performance, with their white make-up, their expensive and peculiar costumes, and their stylised movements, is far pleasanter when seen in a European theatre. And they gain nothing by repetition.

THE ROAD TO ANGKOR

SIAM

SIAM IS an anomaly. It is an independent non-European country. At the time of writing it shares this distinction with Abyssinia, but before this is read it seems to me that Siam is likely to be unique. There is, it is true, Japan ; but the Japanese have shown such talents for organised slaughter that even the Nazis have been forced to make them honorary Aryans ; they would be justifiably furious if anyone referred to them as a " native state " ; they not only have all the benefits of civilisation themselves ; they are willing to bomb their neighbours with it too. Although Siam has a standing army, it is a peaceful state, and, by Japanese standards, fairly backward.

As a country it has been somewhat intermittent. In about the tenth century it was part of the Khmer Empire ; the Thai, as the Siamese call themselves, being by tradition emigrants from the valley of the Yangtze. In the thirteenth century it gained its independence, and in the late fourteenth century conquered and destroyed the empire of the Khmers (or Cambodians, as they are called by Europeans). It continued as an empire till the middle of the eighteenth century ; it entered into diplomatic relations with Louis XIV ; but the missionaries who followed this were so ardent that shortly after the country was closed to foreigners. In 1767 the country was conquered and devastated by the Burmese ; twenty years later the Burmese were repulsed, and the present dynasty formed. During the nineteenth century the country was somewhat modernised ; slavery was abolished, and religious toleration granted; contact with Europe was constant and cordial. In the last years of the century however Siam got in the way of French Imperialist expansion ; Bangkok was besieged, and Siam lost all her territory on the left bank of the Mekhong. Relations were very strained until 1907, when Siam ceded the provinces she held in Cambodia, including holy Angkor, to the " protection " of the French. England did not see why she shouldn't have her share too, and in 1909 threw her " protection " over four Malay states in Southern Siam. Since that date Siam has been allowed, and even encouraged, to keep the remainder of her territory as an independence ; she is a very useful buffer state. In 1917 she joined on the *right side* in the never-to-be-forgotten glorious war to end war ; though the contingent she sent to Europe never actually got to the firing line, a sufficient number died of various causes on the way to permit the erection of a war memorial which is quite as ugly as any to be found in Europe.

Up till the last ten years Siam was an absolute

monarchy, but enjoyed a succession of liberal-minded kings who introduced many reforms into the country, such as universal education and vaccination, military conscription (there was and still is religious conscription for all Buddhists, who for a certain period have to live as monks), and the " Wild Tiger " corps, as well as ordinary boy scouts. In 1925 King Prajadhipok created a Supreme Council of State and a Privy Council as advisory bodies ; a *coup d'état* in 1932 added to the power of these bodies by transforming the absolute monarchy into a constitutional one. In 1935 the king abdicated (it is said on account of his failing sight ; a king should have no physical defect) ; his son and heir is a little boy, and nobody is quite certain what is going to happen in the country ; people around the Court, especially those in important or lucrative jobs, were exceedingly nervous ; for Court intrigue and personal influence is as important to-day in Siam as it was in Europe a hundred and fifty years ago.

The greater part of Siam is absolutely flat, though there are some mountains in the north. We crossed it by train from one end to the other : an endless succession of rice fields, occasionally broken by forests ; a very great deal of water, studded with fields of pink and white lotus, a solid mass of tall round green leaves, almost covering the miraculous flowers ; and smaller patches of water lilies, including the lovely nelumbar, blue and white and pink, standing some inches out of the water. There are practically

The Royal Palace at Bangkok

no roads in Siam, outside Bangkok ; travelling is done by rail and water. The chief export of the country is teak wood, and the north is covered with huge forests ; the only mineral found in any considerable quantity is tin.

There are a little over eleven million inhabitants of Siam ; except for small communities round the capital and in the southern provinces the population is Buddhist, followers of the Hinayana sect, the more " spiritual " of the two varieties. There are still considerable traces of Brahminism in their observances, a relic of Indian and the later Khmer influence ; and the figures of the Hindu pantheon and mythology— particularly Indra—are often to be found in their temples. There appears to be considerable difference in physical type between the aristocracy and the rest of the population, but I do not know if there is any ethnological ground for this, or if it is a result of different upbringing ; the people as a whole are Indian in type, though rather sturdier than most Indians ; the aristocracy paler and far more mongoloid in their build and features. The people as a whole are very attractive, to my taste far more so than the Balinese ; the well-born ladies in particular are the daintiest and prettiest group of women I have ever seen. They are all of the same type, small, with very delicate bodies and small hands and feet ; the face just a trifle flat, with high cheek bones, and large almond-shaped eyes ; the complexion golden and the hair blue-black and slightly wavy. The ladies and gentlemen are exquisitely polite, with graceful and studied gestures ; they are rather doll-like, barely human.

This courtesy is indeed a national characteristic ; their dealings between themselves are a pleasure to watch. As a race they are, I am told, enchanting as friends, infuriating to do business with ; dilatory, unpunctual. English is the second national language, taught in all schools ; there is even a newspaper published in English.

The poorer people dress very brightly, in thin and multi-coloured silks ; the men wear trousers like thin pyjama trousers of every colour ; the women dress more after the European style. As they become richer their clothes become more European ; the well-dressed men wear suits of white drill, very well tailored, and decorated with gilt buttons ; the coat does up at the neck like a military tunic ; it is a very smart costume. The people are very chaste and circumspect in their behaviour ; Bangkok indeed is the most modest large city that I know. The Siamese have dealt with opium in the same way as the Russians have with vodka ; they have made it a state monopoly, only to be consumed on special premises ; and a great deal of the profit derived from its sale is devoted to an energetic campaign against its use.

Bangkok has only been the capital of the country since 1782. It is on the banks of the Menam, a river which is continuously silting up, and creating more and more land at its estuary ; Ayudha, the earlier

The Temple of the Emerald
Buddha at Bangkok

capital, was formerly a seaport, and is now some hours' journey from the coast ; and since the foundation of Bangkok the sea has receded even further. In the modern part of the town there are some fine roads, with European buildings, but most of the communications are still canals and waterways ; owing to the presence of water in both cases Europeans have dubbed Bangkok the Venice of the East ; guileless monarchs have believed them and have tried to make the parallel nearer by erecting at enormous cost and in the face of untold difficulties mock-Venetian palaces and buildings. The Throneroom, or House of Parliament, is built of Carrara marble, imported at great expense ; half-way through its construction the subsoil started to give way, and the building now floats on air-filled concrete pontoons. It is in a sort of Renaissance style, vaguely reminiscent of Santa Maria della Salute, with dome and all ; it doesn't, however, look quite so silly as the small-scale Palace of the Doges built as the residence for some prince.

It is very difficult to take Bangkok quite seriously ; it is the most hokum place I have ever seen, never having been to California. It is the triumph of the " imitation " school ; nothing is what it looks like ; if it's not parodying European buildings it is parodying Khmer ones ; failing anything else it will parody itself.

The Siamese have considerable technical skill, but absolutely no taste. The Siamese artistic canons are

L

" Make it as life-like as possible, twice as big, and four times as expensive." Siamese temples are like a rather naïve person's idea of heaven—say St. John of the Apocalpyse ; but everything is fake, the gold, the precious stones, the jewels, the flowers. The best comment on this theatrical effect is the remark in a guide-book that " the farther away (the Wat Arun) is seen, the better it looks." Yes, indeed. You can't be too far away from these buildings to get the best effect.

The Siamese have also a passion for record-breaking, as far as Buddhas are concerned. In the centre of the town is a gilt Buddha skyscraper, twice as high as a church. In Wat Po is the World's Biggest Buddha, a reclining statue made of bricks covered with cement and gilded ; it is about a hundred and sixty feet long and nearly forty feet high ; it is enclosed in a room and looks for all the world like Alice in the Rabbit's house, after she had drunk the second bottle. One feels the Buddha would be much more comfortable if there was a chimney he could put his leg up.

Sometimes the records are broken by accumulation. I think Wat Po holds the record with something over four hundred Buddhas in and around the building ; there are, however, a number of runners-up.

Siamese in London must feel most at home at Madame Tussaud's. The art which that lady and her descendants have mastered so successfully is the real aim of Siamese sculptors ; unfortunately the climate is unsuitable for waxworks. They go as near as they can, however; and there can be few sights more disconcerting than the Wat Sudat, where Buddha in gilt is shown preaching to a congregation of eighty disciples seated on the pews in front of him like any other congregation; the said disciples being made out of painted plaster, coloured completely naturally, life-size and dressed in real clothes. I presume that during services the living mingle with the stuffed; it gives opportunities for endless imbroglios.

The tableau vivant—as vivant as possible—is a constantly recurring motif in Siamese temples. The finest collection is in the Wat Po; first of all there is a group of the Buddha preaching to five hermits; next a Buddha, about twice life-size, seated on a coiled cobra, the animal's head rising behind the figure with the hood spread out like a sunshade. Finally, there is a Buddha, four yards high, seated under a tree made of rubber and metal; before him a white monkey and a white elephant, hardly larger than life but just as real, offer him honeycomb and water. This group is extremely impressive, but rather dusty. (Incidentally sacred white elephants and monkeys—the latter true albinos—are kept near the Parliament House. The elephants have titles—as who might say Baron Jumbo; only the king rides on them, and then only on ceremonial occasions.)

Undoubtedly the high spot of Bangkok fakes is the Pu Khao Tong, or Golden Mountain, an artificial hill of brick of respectable dimensions. This artificial hill is covered with artificial caves and grottoes, which are adorned with artificial stalactites and artificial hermits ; a few real trees here and there, introduced to give it the appearance of " a real mountain," appear quite unconvincing. This super-hokum houses a portion of the bones of the Buddha, discovered in 1898.

The principle of Siamese architecture is the same as Cambodian, but with knobs on—lots of knobs. Wherever a bit of decoration or twirly-whirly can be fixed with some possibility of its staying put it is stuck on. The hedgehog is the model at which all Siamese architects aim in their skyline. The Siamese also employ two types of tower, vaguely reminiscent of Angkor ; phra prang, or tall rounded towers, rather phallic in shape, and chedi, a variant of the stûpa or bell-tower, but stylised into a steep pyramid with a very long thin spike on top. The phra prang sometimes reach enormous height—in Wat Arun the tallest is nearly two hundred feet high, made of brick-covered plaster in which thousands of bits of glazed tile have been inserted ; the chedi, on the other hand, are usually fairly small, and simply litter up what free ground there is inside the temple precincts.

Most exterior walls are white-washed ; they are the only plain surfaces in the buildings. Roofs and gables are decorated with polychromatic tiles in various designs ; and all windows, doorways, vesti- bules, and so on are covered with glass mosaic to

Compare the houses at the side with
this sky-scraping Buddha in Bangkok

look like gold and jewels, carved woodwork, and wood inlaid with mother-of-pearl. This last type of decoration is extraordinarily well executed; if application could make a work of art these doorways and shutters should be masterpieces; but at their best they are never more than quaint and amusing. In contrast with the tawdriness of the rest of the decoration these fairly sombre panels stand out as the summit of restraint; when isolated they are very fidgety.

Byzantine mosaics show that richness of materials does not necessarily produce vulgarity. There is probably as much gold in the cathedral of Monreale, for example, as in any Siamese building of equivalent size; this cathedral is, I think, one of the loveliest buildings, as far as decoration goes, in the world. With the Byzantines, indeed, the richness adds to the general effect, for we feel that the precious materials are used, not for their value, but for their decorative qualities. In Siam all the fake gold and jewels are used merely to give an appearance of opulence. I have never been much of an admirer of the more precious metals and stones; they are usually too small to have any significance. Until I went to Siam, though, I never realised how appallingly ugly they would be if they weren't so tiny; for the gold leaf, and the glass rubies and emeralds and sapphires were exactly like the real thing, except in size; and the general effect was indescribably garish. Even the treasures of the Spanish cathedrals, and heaven knows they are mostly hideous enough, pale in comparison.

The Siamese love of richness reaches its culmination —and its nadir—in the Wat Phra Keo, the Temple of the Emerald Buddha. This is the holiest shrine of Siam, and stands inside the grounds of the palace. The blue-tiled building is decorated outside with flowers and patterns of gold and sapphire; huge gold monsters guard the doors; golden bells hang from the eaves. The interior is gold, upon gold, upon gold, except for a few indifferently painted panels in the walls. The sacred image itself is cut out of a solid piece of jasper about eighteen inches high, and is of considerable antiquity; it is the Luck and Palladium of the kingdom. It is impossible to gain any idea of the workmanship, for it is raised on a gold altar some thirty feet high; and it has three changes of clothing, according to the season, made of real gold and precious stones. From the ceiling and from the floor rises and descends more gold in every direction and shape; life-sized gold figures, holding many-tiered gold parasols; artificial shrubs made of silver and gold, gold flags, gold lamps, gold flower vases, and heaven knows what besides; and not a single thing, which, were it made in base metal, one would willingly have about the house. Outside is a small farmyard of life-size sculptured animals, holy cows and lions from a giant baby's Noah's Ark.

The Palace is in the same style, only rather more so. The two most striking ornaments are a model of the Albert Memorial in solid silver, and a model of Angkor Wat in solid concrete. There is also a very fine collection of white elephants in bronze. In the European style there are a number of portraits of crowned heads executed in oils ; they are, however, I think surpassed by the life-size bronze statue of H.M. King Chulalongkorn in field-marshal's uniform, which more than justifies Rajadmnoen Avenue being dubbed the Siamese Champs Elysées, or even Siegesallée.

The prettiest things about the palace are the dwarf trees tortured by topiary into fantastic shapes ; and the Chinese statues, which, here and in most of the temples, serve as guardians to the gateways. Most of these statues are of wood, but a few are decorated with plaster and porcelain ; they represent demons, godlets, and occasionally European or Siamese soldiers ; they are above life-size, and roughly carved, most of them rather grotesque ; they have, however, a strength and dignity of conception quite alien to the surrounding work. They were used as ballast in the Chinese boats which came empty to Bangkok to trade.

Some of the most peculiar statues are a group of little lead figures in the courtyard of Wat Po. They are arranged in pairs, in the most extraordinary contortions ; according to some they represent methods of jiu-jitsu ; others say that they are diagrams to show how to stop the major arteries. They might be anything. Nearby, if my memory does not fail, is a model bear's den, which is very efficacious against sterility.

These temples form the background for most of the Siamese festivities, of which there are a great number. At one temple on the far side of the river a fair was being held in connection with some festivity or other. Besides the usual stalls, mostly presided over by Chinese, there were a number of entertainments. It is perhaps not fair to judge either Siamese music or dancing from the performances seen there ; the costumes were slightly fantastic, with very compli-cated head-dresses ; they followed the Siamese mania of trying to appear worth a million tikal, by being smothered in imitation jewels. The dancing seemed very similar to the Cambodian, the music rather more complicated, with no recognisable melodic line. The Siamese sing with a very ugly nasal tone, the voice produced as it were from the palate, with the throat practically closed. The most intriguing performance was a play acted entirely by boys ; I was told that the dialogue was extremely indecent, but unfortu-nately I was not able to understand it, and the interpreter was bashful.

The pleasantest thing about Bangkok are the klongs, or water markets. The western or poorer bank of the Menam is riddled with canals, with small groups of huts interspersed with fields and orchards along their banks. Early every morning markets are held at different parts of the canals, the goods being piled in the boats which act the dual rôle of conveyance and stall ; the marketers arrive in boats and canoes of a variety of shapes and sizes, going from market to market as they do the day's shopping. Against the background of trees the continuous movement is very pretty to watch.

ANGKOR, OR DEATH AND THE PLASTIC ARTS[1]

ABOUT THE beginning of the Christian era there was a kingdom called Founan, which occupied the countries called to-day Malay, Siam, Cambodia, and Cochin-China. The religion of this kingdom was a mixture of Buddhism and Hinduism. About A.D. 400 a Brahmin family from India obtained the kingship ; Cambodia was one of the provinces, administered during his father's life-time by the heir apparent. The whole kingdom of Founan, and particularly the eastern portion, Cambodia, had continuous cultural and commercial contact with China. About A.D. 700 the kingdom of Founan lost its independence and grandeur ; the southern part came under the influence of the Malay Empire, Çrivijaya, which had its centre in Sumatra ; the Eastern part, Cambodia, became an autonomous

[1] In the dating and description of the uses of the various buildings of Angkor I have followed the judgments of M. Henri Marchal, the conservator of the ruins. Nearly every archæologist has a different theory and a different system and I have no competence to decide between them. Through his position M. Marchal carries great authority, and his dating of the monuments in connection with one another seems to me æsthetically by far the most probable.

Victory Gate at Angkor-Thom
Balustrade of demons ‘ churning the sea of milk ’
On the opposite side are the demi-gods

kingdom, very rich and powerful. At the beginning of the ninth century the capital of this kingdom was definitely fixed at Angkor—some earlier cities to the north had before had this distinction—and for five centuries Angkor was the centre of a very rich country. In the second half of the fourteenth century this kingdom was conquered by the Thai, or Siamese ; the capital was sacked and pillaged, and presumably a large part of the population was killed or emigrated. Angkor became a holy place in a distant province occasionally visited by pilgrims ; but the Khmer— as the Cambodians have always called themselves— were too few and too lethargic to keep the enormous temples and other buildings in proper repair. The buildings consequently became very dilapidated, and the quick-growing tropical vegetation, particularly the " air " tree, covered the freed ground and grew everywhere ; seeds or suckers took root in the crevices between the stones, so that the buildings were almost smothered in vegetation, particularly the exclusively Shivaite temples ; the Buddhist buildings, and the Angkor Wat, which was converted to Bhuddist use, were better cared for and sometimes visited. From the middle of the seventeenth century occasional missionaries visited or related accounts of these buildings lost in the forest ; they began to be studied seriously in the second half of the nineteenth century ; after the French took the province in which they were situated under their protection in 1907, more continuous work of excavation, clearing, and preservation was undertaken ; in the last ten years roads have been built which allow Angkor to be reached by car, instead of, as previously, by boat ; the work of restoration and preservation is being carried on as efficiently as the very small amount of money available will allow. Owing to the climate, which has a very heavy rainy season, a great part of the surrounding land is flooded for four months every year, and when the floods subside it is a very hard task to keep down the rank vegetation ; like Alice in the Looking Glass the conservators have to work as hard as they can to keep where they are. The prisoners perform most of the unskilled labour. To keep the picturesque quality of the ruins the woods in which they are now situated are allowed to stand ; although this provides a very pleasant setting it makes the work of conservation far harder, for these woods are a constant reservoir of destructive herbs.

The chief traces of the Khmer civilisation which have been recovered, besides the buildings, are a number of small statues and pieces of pottery, and small metal and porcelain objects which formed parts of various domestic appliances ; and also a number of records, engraved on stone and metal, written in Sanskrit and the Khmer language (which bear much the same relation to the language spoken to-day as Chaucer's writings to contemporary English). These records are so precise that they allow absolutely accurate dating in a number of cases.

Despite the presence of such documents Angkor is

Porch of Victory Gate made of
three-headed elephant

surrounded with an elaborate mythology. The enormous ruins are older than time, built by a race of super-humans ; or, were they built by the Khmers, then these people of extraordinary ability have disappeared without leaving a trace. A film shown in London in the summer of 1935, called *Beyond Shanghai*, purported to be a documentary film about this region ; and the buildings were shown in the midst of an impenetrable jungle (stuffed with the odder fauna of the old and new world) inhabited by madmen and great apes, degenerate scions of King Kong. The person making the commentary suggested that the Khmer were totally destroyed either by great apes, or by people so disguised. My chief curiosity in watching the film was as to how the photographers had avoided taking pictures of tourists, cars, and motor roads.

There are two arguments in support of this myth : first that the buildings were constructed with a skill beyond the means available in any contemporary civilisation ; and secondly, that the Khmer had disappeared like the Maya, without leaving a trace behind them.

As far as the first argument is concerned, the ruins of Angkor, though extremely large, and occasionally beautiful, show no signs at all of any technical architectural ability whatsoever ; they are essentially solid stepped pyramids, decorated cairns, topped with towers. The Khmer never discovered how to span an arch ; their roofs are formed by a series of stones each one slightly over-jutting the one below, till the walls gradually meet in the middle. They did not discover either the Norman or the Gothic arch, which were being evolved at the same period in Europe ; consequently they were not able to make any large enclosed spaces, no big halls or indoor temples. They had considerable decorative ability, but the structural part of their buildings demands nothing more than an enormous number of slaves ; a great many of the buildings are very badly put together. They seem to have learned nothing by experience ; during the whole five centuries they tried to use stones as if they were wood, in the end using structural devices which were quite unsuitable for the medium. They seem to have had no system for measuring land accurately ; their squares, on which their buildings and towns are designed, are at best approximations ; the Bayon, which is meant to be in the centre of Angkor Thom, is a long way out of the straight. The Khmer are technically the most incompetent builders in stone whose work has survived.

The descendants of the builders of these monuments are still living in the country to-day ; and there is no lack of parallels in European history of kingdoms which after a period of artistic creation and domination have fallen away from their own standards and have been sunk in æons of insignificance. This phenomenon is usually accounted for by a myth which I can only entitle the Homosexual Conception of History. According to this legend, when a kingdom

Elephant wall at Angkor-Thom

This wall is over half a mile long; the elephants continue over 400 yards. It is the base of the Royal Terrace

becomes rich and powerful the ruling classes abandon themselves to art and luxury and thereby (!) become homosexual and are consequently easily defeated. The psychological basis of this legend is incomprehensible ; for, besides the fact that communities which have or have had homosexuality as a socially desirable pattern, have almost always been warrior communities, the idea of homosexuality—or even effeminacy—suddenly seizing complete generations like an epidemic has no historical justification soever. I should have thought that the demoralising effect of invasion and defeat and the sudden subservient condition would be sufficient to account for the loss of initiative. There are also many instances of countries staying powerful after they have ceased to produce any art and consequently leaving no records behind them of any importance ; I shall develop later a theory of the historic pattern of art. Finally, in our exclusively militaristic or economic view of history we are apt to neglect three very important factors : disease, changes of climate, and drugs.

The influence of epidemic and endemic diseases on history is occasionally considered nowadays, though far less than is warranted ;[1] although the effect of

[1] Professor Zinnser, in the intervals of airing his views on life and letters, pays a certain amount of attention to the historic rôle of typhus in *Rats, Lice and History*. Although my views on epidemology are quite as amusing and instructive as the Professor's on literature, I prefer to leave the subject to people who know something about it.

malaria on the history of Italy under the Romans has been considerably studied, it is still neglected in nearly all history books. I know of no positive evidence that the Khmers suffered from any epidemics, but comparisons with similar large communities in Asia to-day make it extremely probable that they did. Incidentally I think the studies of epidemology and paleontology could get together with mutual advantage ; the sudden extinction of large species of animals it seems to me can be far more easily accounted for by the emergence of a new type of infection than by the unconvincing explanations (such as the extra-ordinarily restricted diet of the sabre-toothed tiger) usually now given.

Changes in climate have, I believe, been dealt with hardly at all, though Norman Douglas has called attention to the modifications of the Mediterranean climate subsequent to the deforestation in North Africa. In Cambodia I think similar deforestation of the surrounding country must have played an important rôle ; it seems scarcely credible that the Khmers would have stuck for five centuries to a town so situated that it was flooded for four months in every year. Wood was their chief building material and fuel ; the enormous population—there must have been millions in and around Angkor—must have deforested large areas every year ; and I believe that in the course of time the climate became so changed that the country could no longer support a large population, and that those who remained

The Wall of Garudas

This wall is the continuation of the
elephant wall. These caryatides
cover about 200 yards

were fever-ridden. This is certainly the case to-day.

Finally, there is the question of drugs. The taking and selling of intoxicating drugs excites to-day a degree of moral horror completely disproportionate with their social effects. Except possibly in the case of hashish no case whatever has been made out for considering drug-taking socially undesirable ; modern preparations of cocaine and heroin are lethal if taken in sufficiently large quantities over a considerable stretch of time ; the other drugs do not shorten life sufficiently to make any social difference, and on the whole keep people contented and peaceable. Nearly all non-European countries have employed some drug or other nationally ; most of the far East opium and hashish (*cannabis indica*) ; all the near East and North Africa hashish ; the Americas cocaine, or rather the coca plant. Not to mention such substances as betel and cola-nuts, which are not as yet scheduled as drugs.

The continuous use of drugs is employed for the alleviation of intolerable moral and material misery. I think you will seldom find drugs taken by prosperous people in good health whose psychological disposition fits in with the pattern of the community. Drugs are the consolation for pain and cold and hunger ; if they do shorten the lives of their addicts they at least render their briefer lives less miserable than they would otherwise have been. I consider it better for people not to be dependent on drugs, as

M

I think it better for them not to be dependent on alcohol—the European equivalent ; and I believe that with increasing happiness and material prosperity their use will be greatly lessened ; you only want to be " taken out of yourself " if your everyday self is unbearable. I can, however, see little justification in the moral horror surrounding drugs—a post-war phenomenon—which has turned them into a taboo, not to be mentioned in public, and to be pursued with the organised hatred of every class of the community, from the Communist to the laissez-faire Liberal Anarchist. Why, in the name of common sense, is more time and money now spent in preventing people getting drugs than in preventing them getting syphilis ? If the energy were diverted Europe could be free of this socially extremely dangerous disease in a generation. An uncured syphilitic is a far greater danger to himself and the community than a hundred drug-addicts.

The question of drugs is particularly pertinent as far as Angkor is concerned, for I am morally certain that the Khmer were an opium-soaked community. I question whether this alone would account for their complete defeat, though combined with the illness and change of climate that I have supposed the resulting inertia would undoubtedly have contributed. Opium is, however, absolutely necessary for the comprehension of their art. Khmer art has always seemed strange and alien to European commentators ; and this strangeness in analysis is caused by the fact

The Towers of the Bayon

that Khmer art is extremely sensual and completely sexless. In the square miles of Khmer sculpture at Angkor there is not a single sexual figure or group ; the very rare nude figures have no genitals. Many of the temples are dedicated to Shiva whose symbol is the phallus, or lingam ; the lingam are stylised out of all recognition and the decorations as chaste there as anywhere. But except for this sexlessness there is no connection between the Khmer art and the other great asexual art of the Aztecs ; here there is no inhuman rigidity, no denial of the flesh above the bone. (I have only seen Aztec carvings in a few museums and photographs, not nearly enough to enable me to do more than suggest that Aztec art is a mescaline-tinted vision. I think, however, there is something to be said for this proposal ; the peculiar Aztec composition, with the whole field of vision filled so that there is no empty space, the continual repetition of pattern-movement and the sudden changes without transitions all occur in the visions produced by mescaline ;[1] and the discomfort, the insistence on death and decay are allied with the psychological effects of that drug, which was undoubtedly used in Mexican religious ritual. As a psychological basis for this, the most extraordinary of all sculpture, I think the suggestion is worth consideration.) On the contrary the chaste Khmer figures are extremely voluptuous, curved and adorned with an obvious appreciation of human beauty but with no

[1] See Appendix I.

desire. And this peculiar attitude is, I am sure, the result of opium. The following quotation from an American novel, *Sailors Don't Care* (by E. Lanham, Paris, Contact Editions. 1929), describing the effects of opium on a person who enjoyed it—although the book is a novel a great deal is obviously autobiographical—might almost be a lyrical description of the temples of Angkor.

" The next morning he had a headache, but his thoughts were still full of the dreams he had had the night before. He had never had such a feeling of power, of supreme happiness, in his life. It was as if he had been wandering through brilliant Elysian fields hand in hand with *beautiful shadowy* people. Beautiful women had thronged about him, *smiling and laughing* at him, yet there had been *no sensation of sex*, but only delightful understanding companionship. . . ." I have put in the italics to stress the point ; now look at the pictures of the apsaras on the Angkor temples, and consider if they could have been better described. There is nothing in the book to indicate that the author (much less the principal character) had been within a thousand miles of Angkor or even knew of its existence.

These devatâs and apsaras, dancing nymphs and flower-garlanded sylphs, reappear endlessly on every wall of nearly every temple ; smiling enigmatically— surely Leonardo's Mona Lisa is such another, seen with sensual admiration but with no desire, aversion rather—in hieratic dancing poses, kindly and formal

Bas-relief in the Bayon
Cock-fight, marketing, etc.

and inhuman. Every sanctuary has this sensual, undesired embroidery.

Outside the temples, in the friezes, round the gateways, is portrayed the myth which accounts for the origin of the apsaras, the Churning of the Sea of Milk. At the bottom of the Sea of Milk was a flask containing amrita, the food of immortality, only to be brought up from the bottom by churning. In the middle of this ocean is the mountain of the World, resting on the tortoise Vishnu. The demi-gods and demons, Devas and Assouras, determine to try to obtain amrita; they therefore twine the giant serpent Vasouki round the world-mountain and use its body as a cord to churn the sea; the devils hold the head of the serpent, the demi-gods the tail. For a thousand years they churn the Sea of Milk, pulling in turn, and from it arise first the apsara, then Lakshmî, the Goddess of Beauty, then strange monsters, and finally the amrita; but before the demi-gods and demons can profit by their labour Vishnu takes the food of immortality for himself. I will not suggest that the amrita is opium.

This legend is the basis of some of the most successful Khmer decoration. It is shown in one huge panel in Angkor Wat, where the distress of the creatures in the churned sea is very realistically and amusingly portrayed; and all the gateways into the town of Angkor Thom are lined with this legend, the entrance being flanked on one side by fifty-four demi-gods, on the other by as many demons. The figures are

carved kneeling, and more than life-size ; the demi-
gods calm and majestic, with half-closed almond-
shaped eyes, and conical hats (moukouta), the demons
round-eyed and grimacing with crested helmets.
These figures, supporting the balustrade of the
serpent's body, form a strange and dignified approach ;
but for decorative effect Vasouki has been changed
into two Nagas, many-headed cobras. The rising
incurved fan of the angry cobra (the fan filled with
an uneven number of heads, or veins) is the greatest
invention of Khmer architecture ; it is used again
and again, with always successful results, for the
corners of balustrades, for the eaves of roofs, as angle
ornaments. The cobra did for Khmer architecture
what the acanthus leaf did for Greek, or the palm
tree for Egyptian buildings. It set the key.

The mythological figure which competes with
Naga in Khmer architecture is the Garuda, the
mythical gryphon on whose shoulders Vishnu rode.
The Garuda is a semi-human bird, with a man's
head and body, and a bird's wings and beak ; sometimes he has lion's legs. The Garuda, with another
rather similar monster, the winged and grimacing
Asoura, are much used as caryatids by the Khmer.
Next in popularity comes the elephant, sometimes
portrayed naturalistically, sometimes as Airâvata,
the three-headed elephant mount of Indra. In this
form the three trunks are used architecturally as
stalactites, covering small pavilions, or watch-towers.
Before some entrances are figures of dvârapâlas, demons

Bas-relief in the Bayon
Dancing Apsara on a pillar

armed with a club ; and square towers and the pediments of gates are covered with the four faces of Lokeçvara, the ambiguous Buddhist demi-god or Bodhisattva, who in Japan and China changes sex and becomes Kwanon, goddess of mercy. Except for isolated figures, and small decorative reliefs and panels, these dozen or so figures comprise the whole of Khmer iconography.

I think this extraordinarily small variety of figures —compare the richness of contemporary European Gothic—and their consequent continual repetition is one of the chief factors for the very strong impression of strangeness which the visitor receives at Angkor. For the buildings of Angkor are very modern— Angkor Wat was built at the same time as Notre Dame de Paris and later than Westminster Abbey— and yet they are more alien than ruins ten times their age. One of these reasons is, I think, this dream-like repetition of a small number of motives (they have ignored vegetation entirely and, except for the elephant, the cobra and very occasionally the monkey and the fish, the whole of the animal world of the waters, the land or the air ; and from the enormously rich mythology of two religions—Hinduism and Mahâyâna Buddhism—they have taken a dozen figures, not one per cent of those available) ; another is the overwhelming presence of the surrounding and sometimes intruding forest ; but the chief cause of all of this alien atmosphere is to my mind the fact that the ruins of Angkor are completely dead. However fervently you believed in ghosts you could see no ghost at Angkor ; however sensitive you imagine yourself you will receive no " vibrations " there.

We know a very great deal about Angkor and its inhabitants ; there is even a contemporary account of life there by a Chinese traveller, who probably did not exaggerate or lie more than most other travellers —though at any rate on one occasion he was inaccurate—and yet we cannot imagine Angkor as other than an uninhabited ruin. The far more fragmentary ruins of Greece and Crete, the buildings of the Aztecs and Egyptians can be easily imagined in use ; but in Angkor at most the processional avenues can be filled.

There are many reasons for this, the chief being the enormous scale on which nearly all the buildings are made. For us in Europe man is the scale by which we measure, multiples of two yards, when we consider man-made things. Angkor Wat is measured in furlongs, the outside moat being more than a mile in each direction. Secondly, the buildings are almost entirely façades ; they cannot be entered, much less inhabited. They are huge solid piles of laterite, covered with a worked facing of basalt ; narrow stairways and occasional covered galleries allow you to clamber over them ; but there is no space where a man could live, or a large gathering congregate, in or on the buildings. In Mexico the tops of the square stepped pyramids were platforms where people could gather; in Angkor they are covered

Bas-reliefs round a window of
the Baphuon

with towers so that there is no room for a crowd. In the large collection of buildings in Angkor only one, and that one of the most dilapidated, was used for habitation—the Buddhist monastery Banteai Kdei. The artificial lakes are too vast and too ruined to give the impression of any sort of utility. The reason for this uninhabitability is that all domestic buildings, as well as a number of superstructures, were made of wood and similar perishable materials ; according to the Chinese traveller sheet metal was also much used ; but that was almost certainly taken by the conquerors, just as all the iron and bronze fittings of the buildings have been removed.

Despite, and partly on account of this deadness, Angkor is a perfect example of the rise, development, and decline of an æsthetic culture, at least as far as architecture and sculpture are concerned ; the fact that it is dead and alien, so that it has no emotional or historical associations, makes it the easier to study. And, except for the final period, there are a sufficient number of buildings and carvings to prevent the possibility of generalising from too few examples.

I believe that if you have sufficient examples of any form of art developed in a single community over a long enough stretch of time you can always observe the same progression through three phases : the new idea or inspiration (be it religious, historical, or æsthetic) at first presented rudely (the primitive epoch), the development of technique to express this idea as perfectly as possible (the classical epoch), and finally the concentration on technique (the decadent epoch), to give each period its usual name, without necessarily accepting the implied judgments. Usually a historical group only completes a single curve in each art, but there are nations which have completed more than one, such as the French, among whom can be seen two complete curves of architecture and painting, and who show very slight signs of starting a third curve. In England there are two curves of architecture—Gothic and classical—and two of literature. In Western Europe, with a few rare individual exceptions, all our arts are in the final, or decadent stage, more occupied with technique than with content.

In all arts my personal taste goes to the classical, to the period when the technique has been evolved sufficiently to express the idea adequately ; the earlier phases I find unsatisfying, the latter boring. I am interested in What more than How, but I like the What adequately expressed.

To-day in Western Europe we have a completely unhistorical conception of the rôle of the arts, owing to the social position of the artists, and to their insistence on individuality. For all periods, except Western Europe after 1642 (for the plastic artists ; for the sake of simplicity I am ignoring the other arts), and for all communities except the most primitive the artist has shared with the priest the rôle of giving significance and form to the life of the community. In the most primitive communities the

General view of Angkor Wat

artist and the priest are different functions of the same individual ; in West Africa, for example, sculptured objects are pieces of solid magic produced according to the proper ritual ; they can only be made by priests and only used and seen by special people on special occasions. Except in these very small communities priests are seldom artists.

The experiences of artists and those of mystics are strikingly similar. The artist, like the mystic, gets his peculiar experience by long concentration on one object or idea. This experience is for both almost untranslatable into words ; artists write about " inspiration," but they can no more describe what they mean than mystics when they talk of " revelation." Another point of contact with mystics is the fact that the business of producing art seems to act physically and mentally in the same way with all artists, whatever their period, personality, or object. Artists are unhistorical ; there does not seem to have been any modification in the behaviour of artists, when producing their work, in the whole of recorded history. The art, which is the end-result of this process, is dependent on the historical environment of the artist, just as the teaching, which is the end-result of the mystic experience, is dependent on the historical environment of the mystic. Art, like mysticism, is anti-rational ; there is no possible reason for, and a good many reasons against, preferring the picture of a beautiful woman to the woman herself, much less prizing the portrait of an ugly one. To-day, as I have already said, we are at the final, technique, decadent period of art and consequently professional critics—that is to say, at the best, people who have artistic experience but no technical ability—try to explain our enjoyment of plastic arts on the grounds of technique, significant form, harmonious colours, and so forth. This, of course, is the purest ratiocination; if there is nothing more than that in a painting there is no reason why a carpet or a patchwork quilt should not give us as much pleasure. (I must confess that a great number of " abstract " paintings seem to me to be patchwork quilts manqués.) As I see it there is no reason why we should enjoy making or undergoing works of art; the experience in both cases is anti-rational, subjective, inexplicable; I would compare the artist with the priest as a person producing M.E. for the community, and handing it on to the rest through his end-results, as the priest or king does in less tangible ways. For though there is no reason why people should enjoy art, there is very great observational reason for supposing that their lives are unsatisfactory and unsatisfied without it, unless mystical experience plays a very large rôle in the life of the community, as among many sects of the Mohammedans, and certain primitive or protestant Christians—nearly always those sects who have not a priesthood to produce M.E. for the community, but who instead evolve it themselves.

Up to the Renaissance in Europe, and in all non-European communities, the plastic arts were

Entrance porch to first story of
Angkor Wat : with Naga balustrade

essentially public. Only a relatively small amount of painting and sculpture was held privately. Architecture and its decorations are essentially public ; and most of the other plastic arts were housed in buildings that the community used vicariously, places of worship and assembly, churches, cathedrals, theatres, council halls. The Renaissance and the Reformation altered this general pattern which had till then been universal ; artists became self-conscious. The Renaissance caused self-consciousness by resurrecting the art of an alien past (there is no record of this having happened elsewhere) and by affirming that this old art was better than any being done now ; artists developed a historical sense, and a doubt in their own abilities. The Reformation destroyed the sense of being part of a community, by its insistence on individuality, by saying that there should be no intermediary between man and his God, or conscience ; till then the essential rôle of the priest whose offices were shared by the whole community had bound the community together. Also the introduction of an alternative religious pattern into the community weakened, as it always does, the sense of religion in the community as a whole, even though temporarily religious feeling may have been exacerbated ; when alternative schemes are offered there is no longer any certainty that any one of them must be correct. The artist stopped being a servant of the community, often anonymous, a skilled labourer with a very special aptitude for certain forms of decoration ; he became a person, an individual, with no defined place in the life of the community, and under the necessity of making a social and financial career.

At the French court—then the most powerful in Europe—poets had suddenly acquired a very great deal of social prestige ; they were not merely patronised, they were admitted. The painters saw no reason why the versifiers should be better treated than them ; and in 1642 the first exhibition of signed unadapted pieces of mural decoration for sale was held. The painters gained their point ; they were accepted as a sort of gentleman, and they became servants of the aristocrats, instead of servants of the community. The rest of the community either had to do without art, or to produce its own.

This change of status was disastrous ; as servants of a vocal group the artists had to make their end-results pleasing to their patrons ; and what their patrons, the aristocrats, chiefly wanted was self-glorification, flattering representations of themselves and their possessions, or else representations of objects which would tickle their sensuality, naked women, food and flowers, precious objects.

With the French and industrial revolutions the aristocracy lost nearly all their importance and the artists were left suspended in the void. However instead of becoming again servants of the community they made greater pretentions than ever. Religion was sinking more and more into obsolescence, and

Courtyard at Angkor Wat between
first and second stories

religious experience was becoming very rare ; the poets, led by Victor Hugo, claimed that at this period they were the people who obtained visions and produced ecstasies ; they were a race apart, inspired, chosen people ; they and their utterances, which they called masterpieces and works of genius, were to be received by the lay public with reverence and awe. That is true of us, too, said the painters.

During the two preceding centuries the community had got used to the absence of artists ; artists had no longer a place in the communal life ; and although the ever-increasing ugliness of the places and objects used by the community was causing a profound feeling of dissatisfaction (this ugliness to my mind being due to the lack of concentration employed in the making and decorating of buildings and objects) they did not connect this feeling with the absence of artists, and willingly granted whatever the artists claimed. But if the community were without artists, the artists were equally without a community, without an audience, without a function. Except to produce " works of art " they had nothing specific to do ; except in their own and a few other people's esteem they were unnecessary.

The history of painting in the nineteenth century is chiefly the history of the battle between the painter and the camera. The earlier camera could produce likenesses, but not light or movement, or the distortions of personal vision. Until the camera caught up on them the painters concentrated entirely on these aspects of nature, and produced some most lovely paintings, culminating in the marvellous vision and technique of Seurat, to my mind easily the greatest modern painter. But as the camera developed it was able to do this too ; the painter had no function left at all in the life of his community. So they started seeking epochs and places where the artist still had some function ; during the last fifty years painters have dodged from one epoch to another, from one non-European country to another, copying Boticelli or Ingres, the Japanese or the Negro, in a fruitless attempt to justify their inner compulsion to paint. The painter has been left with nothing except his technique.[1]

Nevertheless, despite the fact that the artist and the community had completely lost touch with one another, chiefly through the fault of the artist, the artists' pretensions became ever greater ; people even claimed kudos for being able to appreciate their work. The most astonishing of all phenomena in relation to art is the case of Cézanne, a colourist of genius who had very limited technical abilities though considerable ingenuity in devising expedients to get over his bad draftsmanship ; this artist, with the most exquisite sensual gifts, was completely unrecognised in his life-time, an absolutely unparalleled occurence. After his death he suddenly became greatly appreciated, and those people who had for one reason or another acquired his paintings suddenly

[1] See, however, Appendix II.

Third story of Angkor Wat (Vishnu's Heaven) seen from the second

found themselves with potential fortunes in their hands. This event reduced painting to its most degraded stage ; canvases became tickets in a financial lottery, dealers and critics tipsters. Even one's pleasure in a painting ceased to be a criterion of its value ; a painter one couldn't understand *might* be another Cézanne. And as always happens after a successful innovation followers started copying the mannerisms of the innovator ; Cézanne was a good painter ; therefore all paintings should be simplified for those who cannot draw into cubes ; Cézanne painted so slowly that his models got into very peculiar attitudes to try to rest ; therefore all people should be painted with their heads on one side and their hands folded in front of them. Art is to my mind an essential component of a satisfactory life ; for almost the first time in history we are to-day a community in which art is exotic.

Except for this peculiar modern European development all other groups of artists differ chiefly in the extent to which they look at the external world. The Negro and other primitive artists do not look at it at all ; their creations are made with the eyes shut ; they wish to convey ideas and not appearances. The Chinese, on the contrary, are interested almost exclusively in appearances ; their eyes are so wide open and their vision so unemotional that to us they seem cold and shallow. In Europe we are half-way between these two extremes, wobbling between our vision and our knowledge, tending now one way,

N

now another, at times painting a tree as the splodge
of green we see, at others as the mass of leaves we
know. The nearer art is to religion, the more interior
vision is preferred to observation. As I have already
suggested, the Aztecs and the Khmer artists worked
through the visions induced by drugs, which render
their creations more alien to us than any other, the
only ones such quick-change virtuosos as Picasso have
not tried to emulate. There are, however, some low
reliefs in the earlier temples of Angkor where the
artist, forgetting the visions of the mystic and the
drugged, has used his own observation, notably in
the sculptured galleries of the Bayon ; elsewhere
the observation is confined to the lintels and frames
of the doors and windows, notably in the Baphuon.

The religion of the Khmer was a curious amalgam
of the worship of Buddha (particularly Lokeçvara),
Shiva, Brahma, and Vishnu. These different deities
were not considered mutually exclusive ; on the
contrary, it would seem that they were all worshipped
simultaneously, now one and now another having
preponderating influence. According to the records
of the monuments Brahma was the least popular, for
none of the principal buildings are Brahmanic ; the
other three deities are about equally represented,
though it seems as though Buddhism, particularly
through the mediation of Lokecvara, was the most
popular aspect when Angkor Thom was built ; later
many of the Buddhist temples were converted to
Shiva. The Buddha could wait ; in a few centuries

One of the central towers of Angkor Wat,
seen from the Inner Sanctuary

all the temples reverted to him ; even Angkor Wat, purely Shivaite, became an object of pilgrimage for Buddhists.

In the buildings of the Khmer we have a complete art curve ; in the primitive period the new Idea— the creation of a life of stone, the building that would be a god—executed with fervid enthusiasm and with little technical ability ; the gradual acquiring of technique to execute the conception ; and then, the conception forgotten, the exclusive concentration on technique. Except for the final period, which is only illustrated by Banteai Srei, there are a great number of examples of every phase ; but the primitive concept is best illustrated by the Bayon and the town of Angkor Thom, the classical by Angkor Wat. The Bayon and Angkor Thom were built in the ninth century ; towards the end of that century the builders felt themselves defeated by their medium and for a time reverted to the use of bricks and wood, only using stone for the ornamentation ; gradually they worked out how to employ the stone so that the architectural and sculptural aims of the buildings should be no longer contradictory, but should modify one another ; this experimenting took place during the tenth and eleventh centuries, culminating in the masterpiece of Angkor Wat, built about 1150. This modification was to a great extent the supersession of raised by flat sculpture, the statue by the panel ; after Angkor the sculptured panel replaces the architectural conception, till, in the fourteenth century,

Banteai Srei is a collection of sculptured panels assembled without regard for the necessities of architecture.

It is the original conception, the living building, which gives to the ruins of Angkor their unique appearance. The discovery of soft and easily-worked basalt in a quarry a few miles from Angkor provided the medium through which fantastic dreams could become solid. Every tower became human, looking with four faces over the world ; every wall alive with processions, with elephants, with garudas. Watch towers would flower like lotuses (Prah Khan) ; more, stone lotuses would arise from artificial lakes, with the sanctuary in the heart of the petals (Neak Pean) ; there should be no more death ; the stone itself would come alive. There was no limit to the audacity of their conception. Sometimes clumsily, sometimes triumphantly, the buildings took on the forms of gods and beasts and flowers, cut out of blocks of basalt piled on top of one another without mortar, overlaying a foundation of laterite. There was only one thing against them ; they were as buildings almost completely unusable. With some difficulty the third storey of the Bayon can be reached, but that is so crowded with living towers that there is little place for men ; and in the galleries below there is very little light. The splendid decorations of the town are a triumph—the great doorways with their processions of gods and demons, the four-faced gate-towers flanked by the three-headed elephant, the

Apsara round the inmost shrine of Angkor Wat

royal terrace, six yards high and half a mile long, decorated over half its length with a most beautifully executed life-size frieze of elephants in full panoply, and after that by a series of garudas and monsters flying out from the wall—but the making of usable buildings in stone has still to be learned ; in the Bayon there is no place for men ; and Neak Pean, conceived as a temple floating on a lotus in the middle of a large square pond, fed by four smaller ponds at the sides with decorated conduits—a most lovely conception—cannot even be approached.

I do not think it too rash to say that the Bayon is the oddest building in the world, only rivalled by the Church of St. Basil in Moscow. It is built in what ought to be a square, in what ought to be the centre of the town of Angkor Thom, and was the most sacred sanctuary of all ; in the central shrine was kept the deva-rajah, the lingam which was the Luck of the kingdom. The Bayon was apparently originally intended for the worship of Lokeçvara ; but before the building was completed it was transferred to the worship of Shiva. Its plan on paper is fairly simple ; a square cloister or covered colonnade on the ground level ; inside this cloister a stepped pyramid containing another covered colonnade built half-way up, and the top platform containing the sanctuaries. Owing to the change in the tutelary deity half-way through the construction it was decided to build a big tower in the centre of the platform ; this tower, rising a hundred and fifty feet above the ground, was ornamented with false doors and windows as though it were habitable (a frequent custom with the Khmer) ; and its mass and stress, though it was only a shell, demanded hasty modifications of the original structure ; for on the top platform were already thirty-two towers of varying size and height, every one sculptured on each of its four sides with a gigantic face of Lokeçvara, from five to eight feet high, crowned with a lotus, and supported by a garuda (though this last caryatid has almost completely disappeared). This wilderness of inhuman smiling faces on every level carries the eye through an endless maze and makes of the Bayon a stone forest of faces, a man-made chaos unparalleled in the world.

No part of the surface of the Bayon is bare of sculpture. Every stone is alive with dancing apsaras, offering flowers to the passers-by. And the covered galleries are tapestried with bas-reliefs, of indifferent artistic execution but of the greatest anecdotal interest. Both their workmanship and their interest ally them to similar Egyptian reliefs ; they satisfy our curiosity but not our æsthetic senses. On the walls of the Bayon the sculptors have recorded, rather naïvely, the ordinary life of their epoch.

The Bayon sculptors have the advantage over the Egyptians of being able to portray the human head in profile and three-quarter face ; but they have even less sense of proportion and perspective than the Egyptians, so that a man's head is as big as his trunk, and a fish in the sea bigger than a boat which should be above it, but which is actually below, so that the fish swims in the sky. Now I dislike naivety and incompetence, however it is manifested ; I don't like laughing *at* people or things. Between an interesting thing badly executed and a dull thing superlatively well executed I will choose the interesting thing every time ; I will admire its content and regret its faults. But I shall not try to minimise these faults, far less pretend that they are merits, that such incompetence is amusing. The bas-reliefs of the Bayon are only interesting because they give a great deal of information about Khmer life in the ninth century, that is to say, at the beginning of Cambodia's existence as a powerful independent kingdom.

Naturally under such circumstances war and the preparations for war take first place. We see what must undoubtedly be a series of historical battles by land and water ; the armies and navies passing in review, and then at grips. The clothes and arms of the Khmer and their enemies are shown in the greatest detail ; both sides are very fully clothed, and the enemies have helmets like reversed flowers. The usual arms are spears and javelins and bows ; the leaders have swords. The most important people are mounted on elephants ; and the nobles are followed by bearers with standards and pennants and parasols, to indicate their rank ; the marching time of the soldiers, and possibly orders are given by means of a gong. The boats are long and low, with high ornamented prows, somewhat after the fashion of

the boats of the Vikings ; they are propelled by a
single rank of rowers, massed behind one another ;
the soldiers, armed with spears, stand in the centre,
and battle is engaged by bumping. The most
curious point in these battle scenes is the chariots ;
they are mostly on two wheels, drawn by buffaloes ;
the development and lightness of the wheels and
body-work show a degree of technical skill which the
Khmer have not exhibited in any other mechanical
device. The commissariat travels with the army,
carrying the necessary food and cooking implements
with it. These engagements are directed by a king
living in a palace ; he is waited on exclusively by
women, and has a number of wives and daughters
who are treated with considerable respect. He
consults and discusses with different noblemen and
priests ; the victory is indicated to him by the severed
heads of the enemy generals. To amuse himself the
king plays chess, or else watches the performances of
dancers and wrestlers and gladiators. (It may be
noted that the dancers and the wrestlers of Cambodia
to-day behave in exactly the same way as they are
portrayed doing more than a thousand years ago.)
He does not, however, patronise the circus with its
jugglers and acrobats and stilt-walkers, nor the cock-
fights. The king's food is prepared in large open-air
kitchens ; the Cambodians were apparently not
vegetarians, for besides the meat in the pots we see
people hunting and fishing in the forests. Com-
modities are sold in open-air markets with a very

General view of Banteai Srei

great deal of animated bargaining ; weaving and carpentry are apparently cottage industries. We even see the construction of the stone buildings ; armies of slaves under the supervision of taskmasters armed with whips cut out the rough blocks from the quarry ; the blocks have holes cut in them so that they can be moved by means of poles. To smooth the blocks one is suspended with ropes and swung over another underneath so that the friction shall remove the unevennesses of both surfaces. (The stones were probably transported from the quarry to the site by rafts.) The religious life of the community is the most neglected aspect ; there are occasionally Brahmins, indicated by their bun of hair, among the nobles ; and in mountain caves there are ascetics and hermits. The only distinctly religious ceremony indicated is the slaughter of a bull before a battle, and that is questionable. There are, however, a number of mythological scenes, including a miracle in which the statue of some goddess repels by its magic power the sacrilegious attempts at vandalism by some enemies. And naturally Rama and Hanuman appear ; it would be a strange Hindu building where they did not.

In its form as in its decoration the Bayon is unique. Except for small details the Khmer did not use their observation again, nor did they repeat the folly of living stone. For the next three centuries they worked out bit by bit how to reconcile their visions with the necessities of their lives. They also learned how to build ; one of the greatest miracles of the Bayon is that it stayed erect at all, much less surviving as it has done ; the joints of the stones are placed directly above one another, so that the weight above caused the structure to gape and give ; the Bayon is full of cracks and fissures.

Nearly all the buildings in Angkor are the development from the Bayon to the Wat ; but many of them are decrepit, and in nearly all I think we have only the skeleton. I am not a lover of the romantic ; the mingling of trees and stones growing in and out of one another, so that much of Angkor looks like drawings of Piranesi, distresses me ; I like some buildings, and I like most trees ; but the destruction of the former by the latter seems to me deplorable. I realise, however, that I am exceptional, and that for most people it is this romantic aspect which gives to Angkor its greatest charm.

According to the account of the Chinese traveller in the thirteenth century the greater part of Khmer decoration consisted of light superstructures ; unable to bend stone to their designs they covered the stone foundations with works in wood and bamboo and sheet metal, and cloth and glass ; we cannot even imagine the polychromatic aspect of Angkor with most of what we now see hidden.

Under this superstructure the canons of Khmer architecture were being worked out. Their lack of technical invention prevented them from utilising the interiors of buildings ; they could only span a

A sanctuary and library at
Banteai Srei, with Dvârapâla
in foreground

small roof, even with pillars. Their covered buildings were restricted to three alternatives : the narrow gallery or cloister ; the squat building with a curved roof ; and the high narrow tower of which only the foundation was usable. They did not find out how to equalise the stress of superimposed stories ; the height of their towers is always exclusively ornamental. As with the Gothic cathedral the form of the Khmer temple was gradually stylised ; it was set in a square enceinte, with entrances in the centre of each wall, which were more or less accurately oriented to the four points of the compass ; except in Angkor Wat (which faces west) the east side is the principal façade of all Khmer temples. (This choice of east and west, as opposed to north and south, would seem to indicate that the Khmer, as opposed to the Egyptians and Mexicans, were indifferent mathematicians and had not evolved either a calendar, a compass, or a scientific system of mensuration.) Between the enceinte and the sanctuary were disposed the necessary buildings for housing the priests and pilgrims and so on ; these buildings, where they remain, are all dubbed " libraries," and they are usually disposed symmetrically on either side of the main axis. The sanctuary was also square, on a raised foundation ; round the edge of this there sometimes ran a covered gallery. Inside the gallery the sanctuary proper started, a square stepped pyramid, with usually another gallery half-way up ; on the top of the pyramid were placed five towers, the highest in the centre, and lesser ones at the four corners. The choice of this disposition may have been indicated by the scriptural description of Vishnu's Heaven, with its five high towers.

The life of the stone was gradually restrained, till it became, in the building itself, low reliefs on the walls and occasional statues in niches ; doors and windows were decorated but these decorations were always subordinate and incidental, structural ; the apsaras are the raison d'être for the walls. The Khmer's love of symmetry made them build on occasion false doors and windows, the windows with stone " bamboo" lattices, and imitation blinds. In the approaches to the buildings the live stone was still used ; garudas served as caryatids, dvârapâlas armed with clubs, lions, elephants, and other animals and monsters were used ornamentally ; above all the Naga, with its upraised crested head, formed a structural motive of the greatest beauty for the balustrades. The Naga was not confined to the temple precincts ; it forms the decoration of the (technically relatively competent) bridges and of the landing-stages of the artificial lakes ; one of these artificial lakes is quite pleasantly decorated round the sides with reliefs of fishes and boats which were designed to be seen under the water.

All this learning and experiment culminates in the Angkor Wat, the most perfect building in Angkor, and one of the most lovely pieces of architecture in the world. In architecture, as in all the other arts,

A doorway at Banteai Srei

the greater the complexity, the greater the effect, provided that the complexity does not overwhelm the unity. In architecture we can distinguish four developments of increasing complexity : first, the simple façade ; secondly, the building as a solid of three dimensions ; thirdly, the solid building in relation to the surrounding buildings ; and lastly, the solid building in relation to the surrounding buildings and the intervening spaces. It is this last qualification which makes Angkor Wat almost unique in the big buildings of the world ; space is treated as a constituent part of the whole. This is the rarest quality of all in architecture ; except incidentally in their cloisters the Gothic builders had no conception of it, nor as far as we can see had the Greeks or Romans ; it was understood, though seldom adequately employed, by the Renaissance and baroque builders ; the only two buildings I know in Europe in which space is part of the design is the castle of Schönbrunn in Vienna and the hospital at Greenwich. At Angkor Wat I was continually reminded of this hospital of Wren ; I know of no other building where the solid constructions are so harmoniously related to one another and the intervening spaces ; no other where the decoration is so well subordinated to the original conception ; no other where, no matter from which point you view it, the eye is flattered with a complete harmony, so that even though only a portion of the whole is seen, yet what is seen automatically takes its place in the essential design.

Greenwich Hospital and Angkor Wat are the two most perfect buildings I know.

This perfection makes it impossible to say anything about Angkor Wat that can be either a supplement to or a substitute for a visit. The more perfect a work of art the less there is to say about it, for it has expressed everything in itself. It is by its imperfections, by its faults of execution or omission, that a work of art becomes susceptible to criticism. And since critics to fulfil their function have to discuss, and since they eventually guide public interest, the most perfect works of art are comparatively neglected and unpopular. There are a hundred books on Wagner's operas for every one on Mozart's; there is a great deal to explain, to defend, to excuse, to accuse, to interpret in Wagner's works; with Mozart's four great operas there is nothing to do except to listen. You can interpret Wagner; an interpretation of Mozart is a useless impertinence. Similarly, in modern painting, there are fifty books on Cézanne for one on Seurat, ten on Picasso for one on Rouault; perfection—the complete realisation of the aim—strikes us dumb.

The plan of Angkor Wat covers something over a square mile. It is surrounded by a moat nearly 250 yards wide, crossed by a single causeway of plain stones flanked with nagas. On the inner side of the moat is a wall, or rather a covered gallery, supported by pillars; in the centre is a pavilion, crowned by a low tower, and richly ornamented,

A statue in the wall of Banteai Srei

with two smaller porches on either side. In the centres of the other three sides are smaller pavilions. This porch traversed, the temple itself appears, nearly four hundred yards away, the central group of towers rising over the parallel pillared galleries. The causeway continues, still flanked with nagas ; the lower ground on either side is park land, with two small " libraries " and square ornamental ponds on either side, the building cunningly re-echoed in the shallow water, giving yet another extension to the symmetry. At the end of the causeway the founda- tions rise four yards above the park land, a square of nearly three hundred yards in each direction. A tall pillared portico gives admission to the first story, a covered gallery going all round the building, with a pointed roof of tiles, lit from the outside by barred windows. Over the central entrances and at each corner are towers. This first gallery has its inner face covered with sculptured reliefs, except for one picture of the king who built the temple planning a military expedition, of mythological subjects ; these sculptures were intended to instruct rather than entertain the pilgrims and are mostly of not very great artistic interest. The pleasantest sculptures are in the eight porches under the towers at the centres and corners of each wall ; the necessities of adapting the material to the architectural structure has forced on to the carvers a preoccupation with composition—very often most successfully solved— which is absent in the reliefs on the plain walls.

Except the long and rather monotonous panel representing the Churning of the Sea of Milk, where the figures are more than life size, the figures are small, numberless, and highly stylised.

Between this gallery, the " public " part of the building, and the central block, is another stretch of park land some fifty yards wide, with two smaller " libraries " in the fore corners on the west side. There are, however, three covered galleries which connect the first story with the stairways to the second. These three galleries are bisected by another gallery, and the four empty spaces between are converted into four ornamental ponds. This cloistered courtyard is perhaps the most successful of all the inventions which have gone to the making of the Wat ; the proportions are perfect, the decorations admirably adapted. A number of staircases lead up to the second story, about four yards above the first, and a little over a hundred yards square. This second story consists of another gallery like the first, except that the windows look inwards and that the walls are undecorated. All the ground inside this gallery is paved with basalt, and bare except for two tiny " libraries " on the west side. This bare space is about twenty yards wide, and from it the third story rises up very steeply about fifteen yards, a squared pyramid with three projecting staircases on each side. On the top of this pyramid is yet another gallery looking outward ; in the four corners the roof of this gallery rises to ornamented " pineapple "

A pediment at Banteai Srei

towers, supported by handsome pillared porches and architraves. And in the centre rises the biggest tower of all, it too situated in a bare space, a small sanctuary at its base. Its peak is about a hundred and fifty feet above the ground, almost the same height as the spire of its contemporary, Notre Dame de Paris.

For want of any better method of indicating the proportions and symmetry I have given the approximate measures ; but no words, no plans, no pictures can indicate how inevitable and satisfying is the gradual change of emphasis from breadth to height. The two inner stories are richly decorated with endless figures of dancing apsara in ever-changing attitudes ; the pediments of the doors are covered with more varied motifs.

Perfection once realised in the Wat, the Khmer architects appear to have lost their vision. Henceforward it is technique, and especially the technique of the sculptor which holds sway. Considered as architecture the little temple of Banteai Srei, built some miles out of Angkor nearly two centuries later, is completely absurd. It consists of five silly little buildings, three with towers and two with curved roofs, placed in a line on a rudimentary platform. The forms are those of the towers and " libraries " of Angkor Wat, but they are completely non-functional ; the doorways are so low that you have to bend double to enter. In their golden sandstone they seem less like buildings than like gigantic cruets carved by

o

some Brobdingnagian Benvenuto Cellini. And that
somewhat over-rated metal worker would have had
good reason to be proud of the sculpture which covers
every inch of this absurd miniature ; on a tiny scale
the pediments, the decorated panels, the statues in
their niches, the baby guardian demons are as
beautiful as any of the Renaissance decoration they
so strangely resemble ; the golden stone is worked
like the most precious metal. The Khmer sculptors
a little before the kingdom was destroyed had
discovered all that anybody could know about
the technique of carving in stone ; but they
had completely forgotten what to do with the
carvings.

The history of Khmer art does not, alas ! end
there. Like our own Gothic and Tudor and Queen
Anne it has had an after life in the parodies of unin-
spired executants with a taste for the glorious past.
In the tombs of the last Khmer kings at Oudong, near
Phnom Penh, the curved tower, the four faces, the
Garuda, the Naga, the three-headed elephant have
had a ghastly resurrection ; worse still, in the modern
temples of Cambodia and Siam the same motives
recur in cement and concrete, as horrible as our steel
half-timber.

Herein lies the whole paradox of art. Art is timeless, so that the drawings of our remotest ancestors
thousands of years ago appeal to us as much and in
the same way as drawings made to-day ; but art
is timeless, because as soon as it is executed it is dead.

The art of people of other times and other places, no matter how we admire it, is not for us ; there is no artistic necromancy possible ; we must either produce our own art or do without. Alas, that to-day we have chosen the second alternative.

APPENDIX I

MESCALINE

(cf. page 179.)

MESCALINE IS such a rare drug that my own experience with it may be of some interest. In its natural state mescaline is prepared from a Mexican cactus : as far as is known it was used exclusively by Mexican Indians for religious purposes. When it is prepared roughly the tiny spines of the cactus cause great nausea and distress, so that, it is said, the eater feels all the horrors of death and dissolution. Happily I did not have to undergo this : I was given a subcutaneous injection of the drug, chemically refined ; even so I was, towards the end, very miserable.

The circumstances under which I took the drug were these. A friend of mine, a psychologist, was searching for volunteers who would give up a Sunday to be used as an experimental animal. In the laboratory where he was working they were investigating the derangements of vision produced by schizophrenia, and were making a series of control experiments on relatively normal people with mescaline. After I was injected at eleven I was very unwell with considerable nausea ; I thought, however, that the drug had had no effect. A number of experiments were made with me, and at 2.30 in the afternoon I was left to rest in the common room of the medical staff ; this room gave on to the street, in which there was a continuous flow of traffic, including many trams. By a very considerable effort of will I managed to make notes during the period of maximum intoxication—roughly from 2.30 to 4.30. in the afternoon[1]—and I am reproducing them here without alteration or elaboration. The intoxication continued intermittently for some time after the notes stop.

" Visions like fireworks revolving and falling against dark ground.

Like kaleidoscopic circus with varying perspectives.

Like rather boring electric signs.

Noises come forward like colours ; a moving noise— approaching image as in films (trams).

Great number of neon-signs against dark background.

Rather grotesque and unpleasant electric signs. Paper and hands nacreous (14.45).

Rather vulgar meaningless colour. Iridescent. Luminous. Always against dark grounds with eyes shut.

Cheap *exposition coloniale* effect, luminous fountains, etc.

Paper so nacreous difficult to write on.

Space doesn't matter.

Visions with eyes shut always tawdry.

Open-eyed rather pretty, luminous. Feel very lazy, no desire to move, slightly thirsty.

Trams pass as red lightnings. Always rhythmic and symmetrical.

(15.05) Visions still vulgar. Spangles and floodlight. Cheap effect. Slight headache. Colours very bright, shimmering, with eyes open. Not æsthetically pleasant.

Motor-bike revolving lighthouses.

[1] The numbers in brackets show the passage of time.

Aeroplane noise hurts my throat. Unpleasant associations—street accident (asked if aeroplane 15.10).

Feeling of tension round top of head. Noise like a band (or headache).

Predominating colours with eyes shut red and violet, eyes open green and yellow.

Cheap and ugly version of heaven. Visions and my body are the same. Very difficult to concentrate (15.15).

Sound and light move together. Recognise sounds—they cause colours.

Can see no true green—either luminous or nacreous.

Noise is visions moving at the back of my neck (badly expressed).

Headaches. Noises and therefore colours hurt.

Dr. G. in room.

Skin luminous, frightfully cheap effect.

Tried to concentrate on cedar on lawn—always luminous fun-fair.

Each separated image garish but they change very quickly and [that] somehow satisfying—as though it were my cleverness that changed visions.

Rather unpleasant physical sensations—body large as visions. Noises go through body like wound under local anæsthetic.

I am bigger than visions. Would be pleasant if visions which are part of me weren't so banal.

Klee almost certainly uses or has used mescaline.[1]

Thought (3.30) Dr. G. was also doped. Somehow comforting (quite untrue—he was resting for a moment).

---

[1] This was my impression while intoxicated and it is not altogether impossible. But I should not like it thought that this was a reflection on Paul Klee's paintings, for which I have considerable admiration.

Really very like what I expected from reading.

My everyday perceptions far more satisfactory and *varied*. Hands turning very red.

Would like to see a plain lawn. Continuous movement boring.

Opalescent—like representative opals—so dull.

Cannot control vision-making. Rather nasty (15.35).

Always artificial.

Neither nature nor art.

Nothing sexual in visions—not real enough.

Between nature and art, partaking of neither, inferior to both.

Each return from this unimaginative synthetic heaven harder (15.40).

I-under-the-drug am not wholly I. I think about discussing what ' I ' have been later.

As limited as if living in a colour film.

(15.45) Spoke to other doctors—one came in—to explain how I felt. Now calmer, more detached.

I resent these visions.

Would rather understand professional conversation than have to see these cheap effects. My eyes hurt.

(15.55) Time all right in itself, but other people's actions seem separate, unco-ordinated.

I feel this is degrading. My perceptions are ordinarily keen enough. This is effortless and therefore worthless, also not spontaneous.

My enjoyment is in thinking of the experience as over. Something to discuss.

Sound affects visions but is quite distinct.

(16.06) Went to " urinate." Found it difficult. After much soberer. Will smoke.

Like the idea of heaven of a jazz-band leader—vague

reminiscences of sugary jazz tunes—I am sorry for people who would like it.

Smoke in sunlight first nice thing I've seen.

(16.15) Tingling sensations in arms and legs—insects under the skin—not unpleasant.

Fingers still iridescent.

Sound only affects colours with eyes shut.

Wish this was over. Want to get back to life.

(16.20) First conscious of sore arm.

Definite unhappy feeling. Want to get away from this (? schizoid—more like the *Maniac*).

Time doesn't matter.

Thinking over experience. Feel physically well and strange."

This experience, following quickly after a night of bad insomnia, was my chief impetus for writing this book. Except when I am feverish it is very rare for me to sleep badly, so rare that insomnia, though unpleasant, has for me the interest of all uncommon states. I had been working very hard, and when I tried to compose myself to sleep my mind insisted on going over the problems which had been exercising me during the day. My mind seemed to be working like a racing engine ; the sequence of unsought ideas followed with far greater rapidity and lucidity than is usual with me in a normal state. Had I not been so fatigued I should have been pleased with such satisfactory solutions of the difficulties which had been worrying me ; as it was I wished only to sleep. But my will to sleep was unavailing ; in flashes I saw and heard the sentences and conversations which had been worrying me. Moreover I saw the characters in my book (whom I had purposely kept, even for myself, extremely vague) acting with a definiteness which was startling and slightly alarming. The activity of my mind, or imagination, or whatever it was, was going on without my control ; part of me was lying back, and wanting to sleep, while it witnessed the activities of another part of me. I made a very strong attempt to darken my imagination ; with what seemed like a physical effort I succeeded ; but the odd noises of the country outside my window started forming themselves into a rhythm, which by some association carried me back to the Katchak ceremony I had witnessed at Bedoelen in Bali ; I saw the ceremony again, this time with a different sort of understanding ; my fatigue had reduced me to a state analogous to the earlier but deliberate delusions of mystics ; the peculiar behaviour of my mind, the peculiar ceremonies of Bali, the peculiar practices of the Thibetans as described by Madame David-Neel (I had just read her books) formed part of a single pattern. If I could grasp what that pattern was I should understand at any rate a part of Balinese life.

The interesting point in these experiences for me lay in the temporary dichotomy which took place in my mind. On both occasions part of me was able to note and watch, though it could only very slightly control, the behaviour of another part of me. With the drug there was the additionally interesting fact that (except for my efforts to overcome and to note the delusions) everybody, irrespective of race, age, sex, or habits would with a similar dose have had similar experiences. This was borne out both by conversation and by textbooks. If that were the case there was obviously a large tract of the human personality which appears to be impervious to the accidents of birth and environment, which has nothing to do with the workings of logic and reason, which is, except in degree, impersonal.

I started considering whether it was only drugs which could bring this "automatic" portion of the mind to the fore. My experience under insomnia seemed to show that this was not so, and I recollected that when I and some friends were doing experiments in telepathy and clairvoyance we got strikingly better results when the percipient was very tired or very drunk. It was these considerations which led me to formulate the theory of M.E., and hence to write this book.

It is only under mescaline, and to a very much slighter extent and very rarely under alcohol, that I have been conscious of this mental dichotomy. Although I react quickly and strongly to nearly all drugs I have not the right temperament for most of them. The intoxications of cocaine and ether are for me even less agreeable than the intoxication of alcohol; I dislike being "taken out of myself," having my feelings and my sensations and my judgments falsified : I already lose enough time in sleep. And my inferiority complex is not sufficiently naïve for me to appreciate the compensations of opium or any of its derivatives. An addict tried to persuade me how agreeable opium was by telling me that you have the ordinary dreams of pursuit, but instead of being the pursued you are the pursuer ; but although I understood intellectually what he meant it had no emotional appeal for me. The only drug I have tried of which the results do seem to me pleasant and interesting is hashish.

The first time I smoked *kif* was some years ago in the oasis of Tozeur in the Tunisian Sahara one night when the moon was full ; and though I can never recapture I can also never forget that astounding landscape of palms and mud houses, of light and shadow, the blacks so deep and rich that black without changing its quality appeared for the first time as the richest of all the colours, the pearly white so translucent that I wondered that my eyes could look at such splendour without flinching ; the greys of the half-shadows contained all the colours of the prism.

Some years later I ate hashish in one of the larger European cities. With the concentrated drug the intoxication becomes far deeper ; the whole quality of experience changes ; sounds and colours become confused, so that scarlet is a shouting trumpet, the song of a melancholy flute a pale green arabesque. Time loses its uniform quality, so that it takes hours to cross a room, an instant for the night to pass ; conversation is impossible to follow, for between one spoken word and the next you have pursued so many trains of thought, solved so many problems that you have no time to waste on your neighbour's meaningless stammer. With music every note contains such numberless undertones that the most trivial composition becomes of overwhelming beauty and sadness. For any practiser of the temporal

(as opposed to the spatial) arts such an experience is a
revelation. But repetition is unnecessary ; you learn no
more. And it is in no way surprising that the hashish-
eating people have produced less art of any value than any
other equivalent group.

APPENDIX II

MODERN PAINTING

P. 192. The painter has been left with nothing except his technique.

Friends who have read this book in manuscript have complained to me that the sentence above, standing as it does without qualification, is too downright a condemnation of living painters. I agree that this is so, but the living artists whose work has any significance other than decorative are so very few that they do not to my mind invalidate my conclusions.

The function of the painter, as I see it, is not to give us the illusion of reality, but to indicate through his technical abilities the peculiar aspects of nature which his peculiarly personal vision grasps. An artist should start from nature—the external world—indicating as much as is necessary of his subject for it to be intelligible to the spectator, and so interpret it that he gives to his subject a significance and importance that the ordinary person would not grasp, either because he sees unusual aspects of the subject, or because he can find unexpected emotional or spiritual values in the subject, or because he has discovered unsuspected significance and beauty in the relationship of colours and shapes. The beauty or pleasant associations of the subject the painter uses has nothing to do with the value of the work he produces ; on the contrary, it is far more difficult to say anything new about a rose than it is about a cabbage.

Since the camera was invented this has been the only function of the painter ; before that he was also an illustrator. To-day the only reason for hand-made illustrations is for the artists economic, and for the purchasers an occasion for ostentatious waste. The eye of the camera is a more exact recorder than the eye of the artist.

The realisation of this unfortunate fact has been the prime force in the various experiments that painters have indulged in for the last fifty years and more. About 1912 a frontal attack was delivered against the camera and the tricks and perspectives it used ; the object to be painted was broken up into its component planes and fragments and reassembled on the canvas ; observation was supplemented by analysis ; after a century of battle the painters discovered$_n$ in cubism an escape from the tyranny of perspective and impressionism.

Unfortunately this solution, magnificent though it was, surrendered too much to give to painting a lasting revival ; all sensual appeal was lost, all dramatic and emotional content. With cubism painting became a minor art, chiefly decorative, a dead end. Within ten years all the originators of cubism had abandoned the device as too barren and in varying degrees returned to observation of the external world ; while the followers of the cubists, renouncing even the small amount of observation which was the basis of cubist pictures, refined more and more their statements in insignificant colour and form, until their pictures have nearly approached that summit of pure art, the Bellman's map, a perfect and absolute blank.

Save for a few individuals, to be mentioned later, painting has since continued in the same impasse. Painters had an uncontrollable itch to paint, but nothing to state with their painting and no audience to address. Serious painters

rightly eschewed pure illustration ; but as they had nothing
to communicate they fell back entirely on technique.
They sought to amuse and please the onlooker with cunning
devices.   But technique is not essentially interesting ; if
an artist has got something of interest to state he will
always eventually work out a technique which will enable
him to state it ; if he has nothing to state it does not
matter how elegantly he works. For an artist's technique
is only his way of working ; when we consider a bridge we
are not interested in the way the different portions are made
and put together, unless the bridge is a bad one and we
want to find out why ; similarly with a picture it is the
results which count, and not the means by which they have
been achieved. The only school of painters who have not
been exclusively interested in technique are the Surréelistes,
who, in an attempt to bring content back into the picture,
created a number of literary Freudian problem pictures.
To achieve this they had to revert to the photographic
painting of the nineteenth century academicians ; their
paintings produce an initial surprise and shock, quickly
followed by boredom.

There are, however, a few individual painters who have
worked out their own solutions, who are looking at the
world with fresh eyes. These half-dozen painters are by
no means all of equal merit, and in sheer virtuosity there
are many painters besides Picasso who surpass them. I
only know of painters working in England and France,
and it is quite possible that there are in other countries
painters who have also found some solution. All these
painters have in common the fact that they belong to no
school, that they have something to say about the external
world and that they have found out how to say it.

Frances Hodgkins is a New Zealander. In the earlier

part of her career she made a success as a fairly academic
painter ; she then perceived the falseness of her position
and set out to rediscover painting for herself. Her vision
embraces practically all the non-human side of nature ;
she paints common household objects and landscapes either
separately or together in such a way that the least interesting
objects and views obtain an unsuspected significance and
beauty. She uses individual and very lovely colours and
many of her paintings have the iridescence of mother-of-
pearl. Her approach to her subjects is as impersonal and
unemotional as the Chinese approach ; and in her water-
colours she has evolved a technique which is rather
similar to that of Chinese painting on silk. She has the
freshest eyes of any living painter. Of the other people
working in England Cedric Morris and the sculptor John
Skeaping seem to me to have the greatest interest and
freshness.

Georges Rouault is to my mind the greatest living painter.
He is an elderly Frenchman and a fervent Catholic. In his
youth he made stained-glass windows, and from that experience he has evolved his peculiar technique, with his dark and
rich and glowing colours, separated by black lines. Rouault
practically never paints daylight, or the things which can
be seen by day ; he is the painter of dawn, and sunset, and
deep night, and the artificial illumination of the circus
and the inn and the hospital. Like the painters of five
centuries ago he will place the figures of the Christian legend
against a modern background ; the Holy Family take refuge
in the suburbs of Paris. He paints night landscapes, the
village church tower dominating the sleeping countryside ;
and he paints the most miserable of present-day society—
poor prostitutes, performers in cheap circuses, men mutilated
by the war, the miserable joy of a mariage de convenance.

P

What for me makes his paintings so interesting is the deep
and noble tragic emotion behind everything he paints,
which gives to all his work a significance which is difficult
to parallel without going back to El Greco or the earlier
Italians.

Maurice Utrillo and Henri Matisse have both personal
visions. Utrillo can show the hidden beauty of the streets
and churches of a modern city under sun or under snow ;
this is all he has to say, but it is important because it is
unique ; there is no necessity to turn your back on the ugly
life of to-day ; significance can be discovered in a row
of villas. Matisse is a sensual middle-class Frenchman ;
he uses the most lovely colours to paint what a middle-
class Frenchman desires and enjoys ; a sunlit room
with a half-undressed woman in it, a table loaded with
choice fruit, a pretty little seaside resort. I have little
sympathy with Matisse's vision, though I recognise its
value.

For me, however, the most interesting modern painter is
Pavel Tchelitchew. He is younger than the painters
hitherto discussed, and far more experimental ; indeed it
is as much in the possibilities that he suggests as in his
performance that my interest lies. Tchelitchew was born
in Russia thirty-seven years ago. After the revolution he
escaped to Turkey and thence to Germany ; during that
epoch he did decorative theatrical work. About ten years
ago he went to Paris, since when he has been exclusively a
painter. His very earliest work was superficially bright and
decorative, inspired by such painters as Dufy ; but almost
at once his approach became far more serious, and he has
spent the greater part of the last ten years in experiment
and analysis.

His earliest experiments were in colour. As a Russian

he had not got the European naturalistic tradition of colour,
but the Byzantine tradition of light and tone ; he made an
elaborate investigation of the possibilities of painting in
monochrome, and even without colour at all, in sand and
similar surfaces. His next series of experiments were in
the presentation of a human body in space. He approached
this from a number of angles ; first he fused a number of
aspects of the same person into a single picture, so that
for instance the full face, profile and back of the head were
amalgamated into a single object. After that he did a
series of pictures in which people were portrayed by objects ;
a drapery thrown over a screen or chair, a hammock on a
wall, a collection of objects on a kitchen table, became a
person and a personality. Then he emphasised the sug-
gestions of figures and objects to be found in the drapery
of clothes, in the play of muscles ; till eventually he considered that he had found out how to represent people in
space.

His next experiment was to represent people in air and
light. He did a series of " straightforward " pictures and
portraits, slightly romantic in feeling ; in these he worked
out how to make the picture the focus, instead of the recipient
of light ; that is to say, instead of the pictures being illumined
from some focus *outside* the picture (as in all classical
painting since Rembrandt, with the exception of Seurat)
the picture should produce its own light.

Up till this date all his pictures had been of people or
objects (but chiefly people) in the void. His next experiments were in perspective. Here his non-European origin
was a great help to him, for he had not to get rid of the
classical devices, the perspective of the camera eye. Again
he started with individual figures, foreshortened and seen
from different positions ; after that he made a series of

paintings of " forward " perspectives, so that certain parts of the picture were nearer to the spectator than the wall on which they were hung—a most disturbing effect only rendered possible by his extraordinary draftsmanship.

Recently he has been using this knowledge, so laboriously acquired, for the creation of elaborate and complete pictures. The camera's eye, the single focus, was set aside for multiple perspective ;[1] that is to say, that instead of the contents of the picture being viewed from a single point, varying portions of it are viewed from different angles ; a new world is produced. We are apt to forget that the single viewpoint is only a convention, and a fairly modern one ; in many medieval pictures the spectator's eye travels from point to point as he follows, say, the various episodes in the life of a saint united on a single canvas ; and many Chinese pictures actually require the spectator to walk alongside the picture. In Tchelitchew's latest pictures the spectator scales mountains and lies on the ground ; he sees the people as they appear from above, from below ; the eye is sometimes against the picture, sometimes miles away. Except for a series of bullfights most of these pictures are of the shore of sea or lake, with people swimming and sun-bathing, diving and playing on the sands. The people portrayed have not been selected but accepted ; as in the works of Breughel and Seurat the grotesqueness and ugliness of the casually encountered have been set down without either distortion or beautification ; the world is accepted and given importance, dignity, and tragedy by the artists' treatment. These people are seen in a new universe, seen as we with our eyes five feet from the ground have never seen them ; they are isolated and shadowless ; for the light comes from the pictures.

[1] The Balinese also use this device, see p. 71.

For what they indicate, even more than for what they are, the works of Tchelitchew seem to me to hint at a turning-point, a renascence in the history of painting. With these pictures painting has come out of the studio and laboratory into the world again ; after painters have cast away nearly the whole of the world before their eyes as unimportant to their art, at last a painter has accepted the whole world, accepted it without pity or romance, accepted what he sees. His pictures are often a terrifying comment on the horrors of this world, the poor and the rich, the over-fed and the freak, the exhausted and the mad ; but they look at the world and not the carefully chosen objects on the artist's table or the carefully chosen model in the artist's studio. And because they have accepted the world they create a new world, significant and exciting ; they show that painting can regain the all-embracing importance it possessed four centuries ago. If artists can regain humility, if they can regain belief, whether in Nature or God or Man, there is hope that art will be able to come to its senses (in the most literal meaning of the word) again.

PS.—Since I wrote this appendix I have seen what are to my mind the most remarkable paintings of recent years. They are the works of the late John Kane, who died in Pittsburg in 1934. Kane was born in Scotland of Irish parents, in 1860, and at the age of nineteen migrated to America. He was a big husky man, nearly illiterate, deeply religious, and a first-class workman. For fifty years he worked at every kind of job—miner, builder, house-painter, paviour, railroad employee, steel-worker. From his earliest childhood he drew and painted whenever he had the leisure and the materials. All his most important paintings were done in the last six years of his life. By far the greater number of his canvases are of Pittsburg, " the city he built," and of the surrounding country. With an unparalleled skill he was able to take the whole complex of modern life—railways and engines, automobiles and street-cars, factories and warehouses, skyscrapers and slums, suspension bridges and barges, the merging of country into town, and the dominance of country over town—to record it accurately, and to transform it into a unity of resolved complexity and serene beauty such as can only be paralleled in the two big landscapes of Seurat or the Early Flemish painters. Apart from two admirable life-size portraits there is a certain naivety in his treatment of people which permits a hasty parallel with the work of douanier Rousseau. But the parallel is entirely superficial ; Rousseau was a romantic, recapturing the picturesque, Kane a realist, humbly and thankfully accepting the world he saw.

In his dictated autobiography Kane gives some hints as to what he believed constituted the special quality of his pictures. The first is technically interesting ; he only used the three primary colours to paint with ; he made all his own colours, with the result that he has an unequalled range of subtlety and shading. More important, he knew intimately everything he painted ; he had laid the roads and built the houses, painted the trolley cars and worked the railways ; he had the same knowledge and acceptance of the mechanics and construction of urban life as the studio painter has of human anatomy or the objects on his kitchen table. This knowledge of the world man makes was more common in the age of handicraft ; it can be recognised in the works of most European painters before the sixteenth century. After that the work of his fellows became increasingly more alien and incomprehensible to the painter ; only by regarding machinery as a sculptured façade have a few painters been able to represent it ; perhaps Kane's harsh experience, with its lack of leisure and lack of solitude, is essential if the artist is to regain a real connection with the life of his time and of the mass of his contemporaries.

APPENDIX III

HINTS TO TRIPPERS

I AM *a traveller—thou art a tourist—he, she, or they are trippers.*
The distinctions implied in this statement of the view of
nearly every Englishman or American abroad are among
the most subtle in the English language—so subtle, indeed,
that I am quite unable to grasp them. They are not
economic—witness the way we *travellers* shuddered away
from the boatload of *trippers* who one day invaded Bali as
an incident of their extremely expensive trip round the
world ; they are not concerned with the number travelling
—a small boat was polluted for us *travellers* by a group of
two *tourists* and a harassed guide visiting the Glamorous
Orient ; they are not concerned with the presence of a
guide, for the greatest traveller of us all needs an interpreter
in a country where he does not speak the language. The
most haughty *travellers*, indeed, are those who travel more
cheaply and in greater discomfort than the most despised
tripper : if you travel through China for £5 10*s.* 7*d.*, you
acquire through your martyrdom the right to despise everybody else who has visited that country (you may even make
your expenses on the book you undoubtedly write on your
return) ; how else can you get the true local colour, and
the true local fleas ?

Personally I can see no merit in unavoidable discomfort ;
and I question if you gain anything, except stomach
trouble, by stopping at the local inn instead of at the big

hotel. In places where the inhabitants are used to seeing foreigners your righteous separation from the vulgar herd will cut no ice at all. Of course, if there is only a local inn, or no inn at all, the situation changes.

Another mark of the *traveller* is his secrecy. He is always finding places where there are no *trippers* at all, places which can never be named : and the cathedral is never of any interest compared with the little church in ——. In short I find travellers rather tiresome.

(Another modern snobbery which I find as annoying as the *traveller* is the *gourmet*—I am a gourmet, thou dost appreciate good food, he, she, or they are greedy. The little restaurant which-nobody-knows-and-which-will-only-be-spoilt-if-it-becomes-known is as tiresome as the little village. And recipe-swopping is a sign of the Higher Culture, particularly if the recipes are exotic. I must confess to being slightly tainted with this particular vice, but I dislike it in everybody else.)

On the whole *trippers* are more kind-hearted than *travellers*. The way the poor help the poor is always being commented on : I don't see why the trippers shouldn't help the trippers. To set a good example I am placing the results of my experience at the service of my fellow trippers.

THE DUTCH EAST INDIES

Preparations for the journey. By far the most useful luggage that a traveller can take with him is a knowledge of Malay. As far as my experience goes Malay is the easiest language in the world, a vocabulary of five hundred words being ample for all general purposes. It is a language without grammar or inflection. It is pronounced exactly as it is spelt, and there are no sounds which are difficult for

Europeans to make. It can easily be learned from a book. Despite small local differences it is understood throughout the Dutch East Indies and the F.M.S. Balinese is almost a completely different language, but nearly all Balinese understand Malay. Malay should not be used to the potentates, nobility, and gentry, as they have a right to a very complicated courtesy language. It is very rare for a native of the Dutch East Indies to speak any European language. The Dutch do not encourage such emancipation.

There is no need to learn Dutch at all. There are very few Dutchmen who don't speak English, and those few understand German. Anybody with a working knowledge of German can read Dutch with the following clues :

Dutch UI	German AU	English OW
Dutch IJ	German EI	English long I (mine)
Dutch EE	German Ä	English AE
Dutch EU	German Ö	English UR (hurt)

Doubled vowels are simply long vowels, CH is never pronounced, G is always guttural.

In the Dutch East Indies vowels in Malay are transliterated to the Dutch equivalents.

In the Dutch East Indies the weather is very hot, but the sun, though bright, is not dangerous. Pith helmets are unnecessary ; felts with wide brims—terai—are the most useful hats for both sexes and tinted glasses are essential.

Most men in the Dutch East Indies wear white duck or linen suits. These suffer from the disadvantage of having to be washed after every wearing ; also they look lousy if they are creased. For people travelling about palm beach suits are probably the most practical. Evening dress is unnecessary, but several hotels have large warnings in the rooms insisting on a coat and tie after sundown.

Women should avoid artificial silk or silk mixtures, which perish very quickly in the damp atmosphere. The most practical day dresses are probably linen skirts and silk blouses. A very useful thing for women to take is a mosquito bag—a piece of fairly stout stuff shaped like a pillow-case, which is put round the feet and drawn up over the knees ; this is a very helpful protection after nightfall. Any number of anti-mosquito preparations are sold at every chemist ; they all have as a basis oil of geranium or oil of verbena ; one is as good as the next. Japanese oils will clear a room of mosquitoes fairly effectively ; but they give me a headache which I find worse than mosquitoes.

Laundry can be washed well and quickly—though not particularly cheaply—anywhere ; dry cleaners can only be found in the biggest towns, and they are not very good. Films can be bought and developed almost everywhere.

The object which added most to the comfort of the travellers I saw was a small portable ice-box. Ice can be got at most places, but iced water by no means always. Failing that, thermoses which will keep drinks cold are very useful. I personally find Dutch gin (genever) extremely unpleasant.

Suit-cases which will go on cars are the most practical luggage. It is nearly always possible to leave a box with European clothes with some shipping agent.

Boats. Medan (Sumatra) is twelve hours from Penang and twenty-four from Singapore ; Batavia (Java) is thirty-six hours from Singapore, or five by air. The Dutch lines (Nederland and Rotterdam Lloyd) go direct to the ports in Sumatra and Java ; they are the quickest boats on the route, taking two days less than any other line. We found the Rotterdam Lloyd much the pleasanter ; it has also the advantage of stopping at Marseilles, whereas the Nederland

boats stop at Genoa. On both lines the service is done
almost entirely by Javanese, with a few European super-
visors. Both lines keep the children admirably well segre-
gated. The food was much better on the Rotterdam
Lloyd.

After Port Said the Dutch boats only put in at Colombo
for a few hours, and at Sabang, a small island just off
Sumatra. Sabang is a free port and some things can be
bought very cheaply there. It is a pretty little island with
a pleasant fresh-water swimming-pool.

Sumatra.[1] Neither Belawan Deli, the port, nor Medan,
the town twelve miles away, is of the slightest interest. It
should be possible to get to Brastagi, some sixty miles away,
on the day of arrival. (We found the Dutch Tourist Agency
Nitour, of Batavia, excellent in the matter of engaging cars,
hotel rooms, etc., in the Dutch East Indies.) Brastagi rivals
the Italian lakes as the ideal place for honeymooners. The
country is extraordinarily beautiful and varied, the hotel
admirable (it is one of the only two hotels in the Dutch
East Indies with bath-tubs : all the others have showers
and dippers) ; the climate is cool enough to make walking
a pleasure, and there are numberless walks and rides ;
there are golf-courses and tennis courts for people who like
that sort of thing ; there is an icy cold swimming bath ;
there is even a volcano, Sibajak, to walk up to. The
vegetation is as rich and varied as any part of the tropics I
know, and flowers are (relatively) common. It is in the
Batak country and their most eccentric architecture is to
be seen in the neighbourhood, notably in the village
(kampong) Kabandjahé. The small Batak museum nearby
is an interesting experiment in ethnology ; it contains a

[1] When I give times it is always for what I consider the
absolute minimum for the visit.

fairly complete, though indifferently catalogued, collection of all Batak artifacts.

Prapat, on Lake Toba, lies in less interesting country. Mountains slope down to the inland lake—probably an extinct crater—from all sides in steep spurs. The place of the greatest interest in the neighbourhood is the island (or rather peninsula) of Samosir, which is a Batak preserve. There are three or four old cars and a rest-house on it ; cars and food have to be ordered the day before. They make an excellent rijstaffel at the rest-house. There are frequent small villages along the shore of the island, and a number of stone sarcophagi. The Batak weave, and sell most stridently, quite pleasant cloths. At Balige, on the " mainland," there are some amusing modern stone and wood carvings. The bathing in Lake Toba is excellent— if anything the water is too warm.

From Toba to Sibolga, on the west coast, is a five-hours' drive on a precipitous road with innumerable hairpin bends. Despite its enchanting situation it is as well not to stop at Sibolga, for neither the climate nor the hotels are very pleasant ; there are several very comfortable rest-houses (pasangrahan) along the road to Fort de Kock ; we stopped at Kota Nopan. Fort de Kock itself is an uninteresting little town but there are most lovely drives from there in every direction—to the Harau Cañon, Lake Manindjau, Lake Singkarak, etc. There are also some very pleasant walks.

Padang is too hot to make a longer stay, than is necessary for catching the boat, pleasant. The Medan-Padang journey can be done with a car in from ten days to a fortnight.

To get from Padang to Batavia it is necessary to take one of the little K.P.M. steamers. The K.P.M. have the monopoly of the traffic between the various islands of the Dutch East Indies. Their charges are high, and not all their boats seem to be adapted to the tropics. I did not find the company at all pleasant to deal with. It takes three days from Padang to Batavia. There is a weekly Sumatra–Java air service, but it is not easy to get seats.

Java. For anybody who is visiting at the same time Sumatra and Bali four or five days is ample for Java. The little of interest to be seen in Batavia (the old quarter, the ethnographical museum, the aquarium at the fish market) can be visited in half a day ; in the afternoon one can get to Buitenzorg and see the botanical gardens. A couple of hours by air will take you to Samarang, forty miles from Djocjakarta, the centre of all the monuments of interest. From there it is a short journey by air or rail (I definitely do not recommend the railway) to Sourabaya, which has a small Zoo.

We actually took much longer than this over the journey, and stopped at a number of places *en route*, but most of them held very little of interest. The countryside is far less attractive than that of Sumatra, and the towns are big, ugly, and characterless. Wonosobo has the prettiest scenery. The Kraton (palace) of Soerakarta can be visited on Wednesdays, if a permit is obtained beforehand ; and performances of the Wayong Wong (Javanese dance drama) are given fairly frequently in that town. The Wayong Koelit (shadow play) we saw given at a birthday party in the home of some Javanese in Bandoeng.

Bali. The journey to Bali from Sourabaya is, for its distance, probably the most expensive in the world. The K.P.M. company have practically got the monopoly of the Bali tourist trade ; they own the two hotels in Denpasar, the rest-houses, and most of the cars. They issue tickets at an inclusive price for hotel accommodation, cars, guides, and entrance fees to places where these are demanded. For travellers with only a certain time at their disposition this is very convenient and not unreasonable in price ; people who are making a long stay can probably make much cheaper arrangements.

Bali is so small that there is no object in stopping any-where except in Denpasar. Some people find this place too hot and go to stop at the rest-house at Kintamani, six thousand feet up, and surrounded with almost continual mist. It is as good a way as another of getting pneumonia. The village of Kuta has a shark-free bay where there is excellent bathing.

It is quite impossible to indicate how long a stay is desir-able in Bali. You *can* " do " Bali in two or three days, and you *might* begin to know something of its riches and its people in two or three months. You either love or loathe the place. Many people who were there at the same time as we were spent all their time grumbling—nothing to do, nowhere to go, no golf, no músic, bad food. Without a knowledge of and interest in non-European architecture and art and dancing I suppose the place might seem dull. There is far more social life in the South of France, or in Singapore.

I am told that the country-side is at its best and dancing most common during the summer months.

Angkor. Even now with improved transport Angkor is still something of a pilgrimage. It can be reached from Singapore by two routes : by train to the Siamese frontier, and thence by car (a matter of two or three hours) or by boat to Saigon and thence by car. Either way it takes about four days.

There is a through train from Singapore and Penang to

Bangkok. It is a tedious journey—fifty-six hours in all—and the trains aren't particularly comfortable. Only very few boats call at Bangkok.

The principal buildings of Bangkok can be seen with ease in two days. The town is very hot, and the mosquitoes there are the strongest and most persistent it has ever been my misfortune to meet. They hide in everything and jump out at you at every opportunity. To my mind the most attractive things in Bangkok are the water markets held in the very early morning.

If there were any good cars in Indo-China it would be possible to do the journey from Saigon to Siemréap in the day. As however there are none it is better to spend the night at Phnom Penh.

Both a guide and a car are really necessary at Angkor. The excellent hotel is some five miles from Angkor Wat, and the rest of the buildings are scattered over a large area. It is very difficult to find one's way over the larger and more dilapidated buildings alone. The principal buildings can be seen in about four days. In Cambodia the sun is stronger than in the Dutch East Indies, and there is no shade on the ruins : a sun helmet (or double terai) and early rising are essential.

Fellow trippers, bon voyage !